Pitvc P9-DMR-966

Learning to Live Again

Learning to Live Again

The Journey Through Grief for the Widowed or Divorced

By Sue Carpenter, Earl Frawner, Gene O'Brien, Pal Waugh

With introduction and commentary by Judith Tate

Book design and illustrations by Julie Van Leeuwen.

SBN 0-912228-55-5

Printed in the U.S.A.

Those who bear the mark of pain
are never really free,
for they owe a debt
to the ones who still suffer.
                    Albert Schweitzer

We dedicate this book to The Beginning
Experience and to all those who, bearing the
mark of pain, have reached out to help
others find new beginnings in life.

We are grateful

- to Margaret Rollins who typed, gratis and with love, the manuscript for this book,

- to our friends in The Beginning Experience who have encouraged us in this endeavor,

- to Josephine Stewart, S.S.N.N., who initiated the idea for this book and who, together with Jo Lamia, created The Beginning Experience,

- to our families who gave us the space and time we needed to work on this book.

Sue Carpenter
Earl Frawner
Gene O'Brien
Judith Tate
Pal Waugh

Oklahoma City
November, 1978

Contents

Introducing the Authors

My name is Judith Tate. Six years ago, I listened to a friend of mine dream aloud about a new way to help widowed and divorced persons work through their grief. My friend was Josephine Stewart, a family counselor in Fort Worth, Texas. In October of 1974, Josephine's dream moved from fantasy to reality in a program called The Beginning Experience.

I attended that pilot program and was deeply moved by the straightforwardness of the method and by the evidence of new life I saw in the women and men who came in grief and left in hope. Soon after that, as associate director of the Office of Family Life in the Archdiocese of Oklahoma City, I was instrumental in bringing The Beginning Experience to Oklahoma where I am now the local director. That is where I met the four people who tell their stories in these pages.

Pal, Sue, Gene and Earl are very special to me and to one another. Their lives converged because they share a common bond of grief. Each of them has lost a spouse. Each of them has participated in The Beginning Experience and now each is a member of the team who help make the program available to others.

In this book, they tell their personal stories in a way that demonstrates the major patterns of grief and of the power of new life. Unlike case studies which present bits and pieces of anonymous lives, these stories reveal four very real and unique persons.

Let me introduce them.

Meet Earl Frawner, 35, divorced, father of three children. Earl is a construction contractor who bores holes under highways for telephone cables and water lines. He will readily admit that he is the best borer in the state. Other than that pride, he is self-effacing and shy.

Earl is lithe and dark. That's partly because he works outdoors in all kinds of weather and partly because Earl's grandmother was born under a birthing tree on a Miami Indian Reservation in

Oklahoma. He carries his Indian heritage with dark grace.

I first met Earl at a meeting of divorced and widowed friends. I was drawn to him immediately because his face was so honest and intelligent. And so full of pain. I didn't see him laugh—not really laugh—until months later.

Shortly after that first meeting, Earl came to my office one morning. He stood looking out the window, and I knew he was seeing something beyond the landscape. He spoke of his children. I can't remember what he said exactly, but I remember that it was sheer poetry. He talked about fatherhood, tenderness, heartache. I saw the real Earl that day and many days thereafter.

The real Earl is also a wit and a natural philosopher. Because of his tardy smile and low, slow manner of speaking, his wit often catches people by surprise. His philosophizing ranges from the art of cussing to the meaning of the presence of God in people.

When he was a boy, Earl was baptized in the Catholic Church. He quit going to church when he married and has recently made some tentative steps back.

Earl has prejudices. He doesn't just have them; he proclaims them. He is prejudiced against smooth talkers and people who use unnecessarily big words. He is prejudiced against men who wear earrings and women who wear too much rouge. He is prejudiced against preachy people. Some of Earl's prejudices are obvious as he tells his story in this book. Also obvious in the telling are his wit, honesty and earthy poetry.

Meet genteel Pal Waugh, 61, widowed, mother of five children, devout Lutheran. Pal's given name is Opal, a name she doesn't like. Her father dropped the "O" and the change seems to point up the coziness characteristic of Pal.

When I first met Pal, she struck me as very proper. Almost Victorian. I imagined that, when she was a child, she probably wore white pinafores and took private piano lessons. Her laugh is richly modulated and causes me to think she studied elocution in school.

I don't know about the white pinafores, but I do know that Pal is, in fact, a cultured and proper person. And I quickly learned something else about this fine woman. We were sitting with a small group of men and women who had lost their spouses. One woman involved in a live-together arrangement for eight years talked about her despair now that the affair was over. I glanced at Pal to see if she was shocked. In a way, she was. But the face she turned toward that woman was so full of compassion there was no space left for condemnation. I realized then that Pal, secure in her own moral values, doesn't have to bolster them by casting stones or pointing fingers.

Pal is both Opal and Pal in temperament. Her home shows this. As Opal, she makes her home comfortable with big cushions, oil paintings, knickknacks and a piano. Her yard is inviting with old-fashioned flower beds and curved walks. As Pal, she comes rushing in late and breathless to most meetings, blond-grey hair a bit disheveled and notes falling in disorder from her purse and notebook.

More Opal than Pal shows in her writing as she tells her story in these pages.

Meet 100-pound Sue Carpenter, 33, divorced, mother of four children, Catholic. Sue is pale and blond. Her tininess and paleness cause her to appear fragile, if not downright weak. But she isn't. I have noticed her strength in her walk (full weight firmly on each foot) and in her voice (rich in overtones).

I first met Sue by phone. She wanted to attend a program I was directing for divorced persons, and I thought she wasn't ready. She spoke in an even voice, almost a monotone. Only the timbre of it alerted me to the heavy pain she bore. She was persistent about coming, and I finally relented.

I remember noticing her glasses. They kept slipping down to the end of her nose, and she would push them up with such an impatient gesture that I wondered how they had the nerve to slide back down. I wouldn't say the glasses gave Sue an owlish look, but they made her seem wise.

And Sue is wise. Not just because she is very bright, but also because she has been a sister to pain since childhood; and she has coped. Coping has been hard for Sue because she has lacked trust in herself and in others. But determination seems to rise from some mysterious well inside her.

I notice voices a lot. When I first met Sue, she spoke in a brittle voice. Each word seemed to be chiseled and square. Nowadays she speaks more smoothly and with frequent glints of laughter.

Sue is afraid of self-pity. She tells her story with a kind of sensitive detachment.

Meet Gene O'Brien, 52, widowed, father of five daughters. Gene's face is like a book. One can read innocence in its youthful smoothness (He could pass for 40!) and suffering in its few deep creases. They are honest creases which do double duty: Laughter runs in them as naturally and easily as pain and sympathy.

Gene epitomizes the regular life. He has lived in the same house for 21 years, driven the same car for 10 years and worked at the same desk for 27 years. He often ushers at the 8:30 Mass on Sunday. He is one of those pillar-of-the-parish type of Catholics.

My first impression of Gene was that he was habitually unperturbed. It seemed as if order and routine had created a thick-walled vessel into which Gene poured his life. When Gene's wife died, he put his grief into that vessel and, from outward appearances, his grief burned briefly and then cooled against the order of life. Not so.

If Gene had "acted out" his grief, it would not have raged so bitterly inside him. As it was, the vessel in which Gene carried his loss intensified the pain.

One thing I have noticed about this man is that he is always "simply Gene," whether he is distributing church bulletins in a suit and tie or doing a jig on stilts at a picnic. Gene is Gene. No masks for this man.

Gene is a romantic. He expresses himself in images and tends to use long, flowing sentences.

His gentle authenticity and romantic imagery, his faith and self-discovery color the story of himself that he tells in these pages.

Pal, Sue, Gene, and Earl most likely would have worked through their grief without The Beginning Experience. But participating in the program helped them move more quickly and thoroughly toward new life.

The Beginning Experience is a weekend program which helps divorced and widowed persons work through their grief, make a firm and gentle closure on the past and move into a new beginning. Two major patterns undergird the program. One is the psychological pattern of the grief process and the other is the theological pattern of pain-death-resurrection.

Grief is as old as human history. Ever since human beings have been capable of feeling attachment, they have been vulnerable to loss and to the sorrow that attends significant losses.

Although grief is an ancient human experience, its patterns and effects have been studied only in the past three or four decades. These studies indicate that grief is not a single emotion but a cluster of emotions and they work in a *process*.

The Beginning Experience helps people both to understand the process and to work through their grief more quickly and more thoroughly than they otherwise might.

Grief can be so prolonged that, when people finally finish with it, they are too exhausted to move on into life with energy. The Beginning Experience telescopes the grief process in such a way that it becomes clear and intense. The program's very intensity is like a magnet which draws people steadily through the stages of grief and helps them come to full acceptance.

The program also helps people work through their pain with a kind of tidy thoroughness. Grief is so amorphous that, even after people have passed through it, they are apt to find some traces lingering in their lives. They may, for instance, let go of anger and find remedies for loneliness but still suffer from lack of trust.

That is the psychological pattern of The Beginning Experience. The theological process on which it is built is the pattern of pain-death-resurrection.

I used to think that resurrection referred to something that happened to Jesus Christ 2,000 years ago or to something that could happen to me at the end of life. Lately, however, I've come to realize that resurrection is that—and more than that. It is an *ongoing* mystery in my life and in the lives of all the Sues, Genes, Earls and Pals. That mystery is simply this: Since God lives in us, we have *in us* the power of new life.

Grief is an agony. It's a kind of emotional death. If we pass through it, we can come to new life. We can do that because God-in-us raises us up. Over and over again.

During The Beginning Experience weekend, many people—all bearing the mark of pain—gather together. The intensity of that much pain ushers in the courage and energy necessary to embrace a new beginning to a new life. That is resurrection.

I mentioned earlier the straightforwardness of the program. I think that directness lies in the lack of lecture and the use of personal sharing. Another term for this method is "story psychology." Lectures involve us primarily on the intellectual level. Personal and real stories involve our hearts, emotions and imaginations. We still use our minds to ask ourselves about the meaning of the story and the story's relation to our own lives. But we also enter into the story. We experience the story. And in that very process, we begin to refashion the story of our own lives.

People who get in touch with their own stories can then make some changes. In professional parlance, this is sometimes called "soul-making."

Earl and Gene, Pal and Sue use this method of personal sharing in this book. Their stories are not meant to be models of right behavior or of the "proper" approach to grief. Their stories simply relate how *they* experienced the death of their own marriages, worked through their grief, and sought to make a new beginning with new-life qualities. The value of their stories lies, I think, in their unedited honesty.

I know that it has not been easy for them to say all they have said in this book. I also know that they have said it all with the hope that their stories might encourage those who have lost a spouse and enlighten those who need to understand.

1. Working Through Grief

Loss is generally announced in ordinary events on ordinary days. There is no change in the background music to alert people that their lives are about to shatter. It comes while they drink a glass of water or smoke a cigarette. Their initial response to the announcement of loss is disbelief, or denial. Denial cushions the impact. It keeps the blow from striking their hearts with too much force too suddenly.

When loss is grievous, as it is in the loss of a spouse, it thrusts people into that welter of emotion called *grief.* Denial is one of grief's first emotions. Other emotions include anger, shame, guilt, bitterness, blame, hatred and depression. As these feelings come colliding against each other, people are thrown headlong into first one emotion, then another, and then into several emotions at once.

They are tossed back and forth. For grief has no order. And no schedule. If the sufferers could say, "Now I am in the stage of anger and have only two more stages to go," they would find the whole experience more tolerable. But they cannot do that. It is precisely the intensity of the feelings and their disorder that makes grief almost unbearable. Grief is indeed a jagged journey.

Even though there is no clearly ordered process in the actual experience of grief, four general patterns emerge which can be labeled as denial, anger, bargaining and depression.

The initial denial is characterized by shock and disbelief. "There is some mistake." "She doesn't mean what she is saying." "I'm dreaming all this."

Later, when the facts force persons to a rational admission of their loss, they nevertheless seek an emotional denial. Numbing feelings is one form of emotional denial. Some typical ways people deaden feelings are to work into a stupor of fatigue, to drink themselves into Never-Never Land, to steel themselves behind a mask of strength that doesn't allow feelings, to stay in shock so they won't have to move on into the pain, or to cop out by turning it all over to the Lord as if he is some kind of cosmic anesthetist.

Hurt people can use such denial strategies to battle against their pain not only at the onset of grief but also later during the grief process.

Another grief reaction is sometimes described as bargaining. Actually, bargaining is another form of denial that the loss is real. It's a way of pretending that the loss isn't a loss but just the threat of a loss.

People might try bargaining with God: "I'll give $500 to the Church if you let him recover from the surgery." "If you'll fix up this marriage, I'll be a more loving husband."

They can also bargain with their spouse: "Stay with me and I promise to change." "Don't die and leave me now."

Finally, they can bargain with themselves, not in order to avoid the loss but in order to avoid the pain: "If I pray, it won't hurt." "If I move, I can forget." "If I change my values, I won't be so lonely."

Bargaining is one of the most subtle and, at the same time, one of the most painful grief emotions. It is painful because it is hopeless. Down deep, bargainers know it is unrealistic. Perhaps its hopelessness is the reason bargaining usually doesn't last long on the battlefield of grief.

Another set of grief emotions centers on anger. In 20th-century America, it is okay to be shocked. It is even okay to be hurt if the people who are hurting don't make too big a scene. But it is seldom okay to feel anger—or, at any rate, to show it. Yet anger is an essential part of grief. It comes, willy-nilly, crashing into the other grief emotions, tearing people and blinding them.

Since anger is often unacceptable and since it will almost certainly come, it often has to come disguised. Grieving people disguise anger in two ways: by giving it an acceptable label and by diffusing it.

If saying "I feel angry" is unacceptable, angry people can say they feel cheated, guilty, betrayed, abandoned or ashamed. These feelings are "permissable." Behind such labels anger tries to work out its rage. It would, perhaps, be a simpler and shorter process if they claimed anger as anger without trying to change it into something else. For whatever they call it, the fact remains that anger is almost always part of grief.

Another way to cloak anger is to diffuse it, to lose track of it. This isn't too difficult since the anger which accompanies grief is inclined to go in several directions at once.

People who lose a spouse can aim some of their anger at God for letting the loss occur, some against their former spouses for causing their hurt, some toward themselves for behaving in ways that brought about their loss.

They can also send anger out in the vague direction of "others." It can be diffused among all kinds of people: couples who are still happily married, doctors who should have saved the spouse's life, relatives who should be more understanding, lawyers who take advantage of the grieving person's single-again situation, clergy who exclude or ignore them.

Or, finally, they can just be angry at the situation.

The last painful set of grief emotions is depression. In depression, grieving people no longer deny their loss. They simply hurt and cannot stop hurting.

When they wake up, they discover that pain has been with them all night and is waiting to drag them through another day. They have no energy. Sadness envelops them like a climate. They see others walking in sunshine but they walk in shadow. Sometimes they cry; but more often their tears, unshed, form a stony lump that keeps their breath shallow and their hearts heavy. If someone extends a hand to them, they scarcely have the energy or the will to take it.

Like the other grief emotions, depression has degrees of intensity. It can range from vague sadness to suicidal despair. It is probably the most frightening and lonely of all the grief emotions. Since people could not bear undiluted depression for a very long time, the very disorder of the grief process, otherwise so frustrating, actually becomes helpful during depression. Feelings like anger and guilt at least bring some relief and distraction.

Denial, anger, bargaining and depression are the major grief emotions. The only way grieving people can come to final acceptance and new life is to *work through* these emotions. If they try to work around the feelings or skip over them, they will not really resolve their grief.

What does "working through" grief mean? It means to lean into the pain, to let oneself hurt; it means to talk, to put words around the feelings; it means to feel and taste and show the shock, the outrage, the sadness.

If hurt people do not work through their grief, they are likely to push the unresolved feelings down inside themselves where, like an infection, grief will spread into other areas of their lives.

Some indications that unresolved grief is still at work in people include chronic boredom, self-pity, self-hatred, distrust, promiscuity, overwork, temper and frenzied activity. They key word here is *chronic;* these behaviors indicate unresolved grief only when they are more or less habitual.

Grief is ugly. The journey through it is

excruciating. When people have worked through it, they will bear scars. But they will also feel cleansed, unburdened and full of hope. For strange as it may seem, people who travel this jagged road are almost always enriched. They are more realistic, more compassionate, more profoundly human. In short, they are nearly always more beautiful than they ever could have been before traveling through grief.

Gene's Story

The reunion had been in the planning stages for a long time, but at last all obstacles had been cleared. The three sisters were now going to be able to spend four carefree and fun-filled days together, relaxing and visiting. They had even planned a day-long side trip from Lubbock, the city in west Texas where Anna Margaret lived. Virginia was coming from Hoffman Estates, a Chicago suburb, and would meet Blanche on a connecting flight so they could arrive at Lubbock together. It was going to be an exciting time.

The weather was cold in Oklahoma City that Wednesday night as my wife, Blanche, closed our back door behind her as she had done thousands of times before. We chatted on the way to the airport about ordinary, everyday things—about the need to pick a bouquet of chrysanthemums before the hard freeze ruined the blooms, about the fine turkey she had bought just that day for

Thanksgiving, and about the good times we would have as our family celebrated the coming holidays.

Before we knew it, it was boarding time for her flight to Lubbock. I quickly gave her my standard "public" kiss and teasingly told her I'd try not to forget to meet her there when she returned Sunday night.

As she started down the boarding ramp to the plane, she turned slightly and gave me her familiar little wink. Over the years I had come to know that special gesture meant she felt good. She was happy, and I was part of the reason why. That last expression of her love will always be deeply imprinted on my mind.

I was totally unprepared for the devastating event less than 48 hours later that so suddenly changed the life-style I had known and loved for 25 years. With no action on my part nor any forewarning whatsoever, I was shoved into the depths of frustration and grief as the result of an automobile accident that took the life of the one person I loved most of all, my wife.

Just a few months before, Blanche and I had celebrated our silver wedding anniversary, and it was a most special occasion for us. We had taken a leisurely trip and, for a few days, we were the only two people on earth. It had been a time of the outpouring of our love, of reliving memories, of feeling the joy in our marriage and in our five daughters. Our pledges of mutual trust and love had survived the years untarnished, and the really tough sacrifices were basically over. We congratulated ourselves on a job well done. The first 25 years were supposed to be the hardest, and we had made it!

We had no doubt that in 25 more years we would be celebrating our golden anniversary, and we had envisioned what old age together would be like. We would have the freedom to do as we pleased, the responsibilities would be lessened and our grandchildren-to-be would delight us. The future looked so good that we awaited it with open arms.

Little did we know or suspect then that we were celebrating our last anniversary together; that there would be no more Christmases for us, or that she would never hold a single grandchild. A car out of control in a blinding snowstorm in west Texas and a broadside collision saw to that. At the moment of impact, a pleasurable trip became a nightmare for the families involved and ended much too soon the life of this beautiful person with whom I have had the privilege of sharing more than half my life. At Blanche's death, all the plans and dreams we had so carefully made died right along with her, and I felt that a lot of me died too.

Because of the storm, the desolate area where the accident occurred and the confusion at the scene, it was not immediately known for certain that it was Blanche who had died. The injured were taken to hospitals in three different towns, purses were mixed up, and the Texas Highway Patrol would give no information until positive identification could be made.

My brother-in-law in suburban Chicago was contacted by the hospital, and from the description they gave him, he concluded it was Blanche who had been killed. He had tried unsuccessfully to phone me and, in desperation, had called the rectory of our parish. Father John, the young priest who answered the phone, was stunned by the message, for he knew Blanche and me very well. In a matter of a few minutes he was standing in my living room.

I knew Father John to be a completely honest man, but I couldn't bring myself to believe what he was telling me. Such a thing couldn't be true. I just knew a terrible mistake had been made and it would get corrected shortly. After all, things like this happened to strangers; there was no way this could be happening to the O'Brien family. It just didn't make sense.

The first indication that I was right came an hour or so later when I received my first phone call from a highway patrolman. He told me there had been a death in that accident, but they were unable to identify the victim. He told me I should draw no conclusions—good or bad—until it could be determined for certain who had died.

I had a ray of hope! But I really didn't know what to hope for. I had no doubt now that there had been a death, but I would not allow myself to believe it could be Blanche.

I had some time though—time to make a deal. I just knew the God that Blanche and I loved would set everything straight. I had several proposals that he couldn't refuse, for after all, he was really going to benefit a lot from them in the long run.

That first night was a hodge-podge of thinking, praying, bargaining and begging. Oh, how I begged that what I had heard was all wrong.

Sometime during that long night a spark of rational thinking hit me. Why hadn't I thought of it before? I knew what I could do the first thing in the morning to end this terrible waiting and wondering. I could call the funeral home in that distant town and have them describe the wedding ring to me. And this I did.

I tried to brace myself for what I might hear, but still I wasn't ready when I heard it. The words read to me that morning by some stranger were the same words I had had inscribed in the ring 25 years earlier: "To Blanche from Gene" and our wedding date, "1-27-51." He also described the clothes she was wearing—the becoming outfit she had purchased for her trip and had modeled for me just the weekend before.

I will never forget the feeling of despair and helplessness that seized me and the chill that caused me to shake all over. I had made that call while sitting on our bedroom floor, and as I hung up the phone, I started pounding the floor with my fists!

I lashed out at God for doing this to us: "Well I hope you're satisfied now. You weren't content to leave us alone in our happiness, were you? It seems like you've always got to deal out some misery when things are going well. I've seen it happen to lots of others, and I don't understand."

I kept asking him over and over again why it had to be this way. There was no good reason for this to happen. The God I had loved and trusted had betrayed me. He had suddenly destroyed Blanche's and my life and doomed me to struggle on without her companionship and love. It seemed so unfair— to her, to our children and to me.

I was completely helpless to change anything. For the first time since I had been told of the accident, I began crying. Depression overpowered me.

Because of the storm, it was nearly three days before they could return her body to Oklahoma City, and during those long days and sleepless nights, my grief jumped back and forth between anger and denial, then depression—and even some bargaining still. For after all, I had not yet seen for myself—and I had heard of monumental mistakes.

The time came when I could no longer delude myself. I saw her, and it was all true. There had been no mistake. No more use in begging or bargaining anymore, for the last parcel of hope was gone.

The suddenness of Blanche's death did not permit me to stay very long in the denial or bargaining stages of my grief, nor, for that matter, in the anger stage either. I was very fortunate to have the support and direction of this most caring young priest, my friend John. He was the one who first brought me the news of Blanche's death, and he was the one who helped me realize I was not alone in my suffering. Christ himself, the Son of God, had not been exempt from suffering and a death that made no sense to the human mind. In fact, he had experienced some of the same grief feelings I was having. His acceptance was the beginning of the new life he brought to us through his resurrection.

My mind rationalized that Blanche was gone all right; and I accepted that reality. But emotionally, I had a difficult time with it. My emotional resistance hung on in the form of depression, and I seemed stuck there.

Prior to Blanche's death I had been a basically happy person. I had looked forward to each new day and to making plans for the future. I had felt good about myself, and I did not take life too seriously.

After her death, I changed. I was not only sad and lonely, but I also became edgy and unhappy. Little things that I hardly noticed before were all of a sudden of prime importance. I began to lash out at my kids for the slightest reason. If the dishes weren't stacked in the dishwasher properly, I let them know it! My shirts were too wrinkled; the radio was turned up too high; they talked too long on the telephone; they were slow getting up in the morning and slow to get to bed at night. Hell, I was even fussing at them just because the phone rang so often.

I was also bitter about being forced into the unfamiliar new role of running the household. I hated to shop for groceries and plan meals day after day. I hated clothes shopping with my daughters, playing chauffeur, doing all the million and one things that Blanche could do so easily to make our home life smooth.

I felt washed out and empty of ambition. I didn't like what had happened to me, and what was worse, I didn't like *me*, either! Life seemed so futile now and I didn't want to think about any future. I was dying an emotional death of my own, and I just didn't care much anymore.

Earl's Story

The words that Nancy spoke to me were calm and deliberate. As I stood there looking at the phone, I knew I was in for a lot of misery.

The conversation started as it did every night, with light talk. And then it turned suddenly serious when she said I was overdrawn at the bank and was late on some equipment payments. That news was not totally unexpected, but still I was in no mood to hear any more about it. I knew that in one week the job I was working on would be completed and I would have all the money I needed to catch up. These thoughts were going through my mind as Nancy kept talking, and I almost missed what she said next: "I don't want to live with you any more."

A sudden sick feeling was in my stomach and I felt my shoulders sag as if a good amount of weight was added to them. I was numb and speechless. It was nine o'clock at night and she was three hundred miles away. I told her not to say anything more, that I would be home as soon as possible.

On that drive home, I thought of the things I would tell her. I would tell her that I loved her—something I had not said for eight years.

Eight years before Nancy had divorced me for one day. She had said then that she didn't love me and that the only reason she had ever said she did was because I made her say it. I had been hurt, and I determined never to make her say it again. If I wouldn't tell her I loved her, she wouldn't feel like she had to say she loved me. I did slip once, one night while making love. But that was the only time

I said it in eight years.

Driving home I realized how childish I had been. It was a game we had played, and a cruel game it was. I decided that when I got home, I would express my feelings for her in a way I had never done before.

During that drive home I started having a lot of negative feelings about myself. We had gotten back from Alaska only seven months before. The six months we spent there ended in financial disaster. I lost all that I had made in the previous five years.

Going to Alaska had been a childhood dream. It was my dad's dream, and he never made it. So when I had the opportunity to go, I sold my business and left with dreams of making my fortune. I think I could have made it, but Nancy was so unhappy there that I decided to come back. We came home penniless. It had been my decision to go, so I had to blame myself for the outcome.

During the seven months we had been back, I had not shown myself any mercy at work. I was working 90 hours a week, and I didn't intend to let up until I had regained all that we had lost.

I decided that when I got home, I would tell Nancy not only that I loved her very much but also that I would soon make her a rich woman. While I was at it, I would tell her I would stop gambling. I had gambled ever since I was a boy; and the more I won, the more I bet. When I would lose, Nancy would be upset. So I would quit.

With all these proposals in my head, I began to feel a lot better because there just wasn't any way she could turn me down.

I was wrong. When I got home, I felt the misery and heartache so deep down that I knew it would be a long time before I was rid of it.

My wife didn't love me. That was the reason for my divorce. She said that I was a good person, a good father and a good provider, and that it didn't seem right for me to have to go through life with someone who didn't care for me. Her words came out as soft as possible, but they were too hard for me to take.

I tried to convince Nancy that I really didn't require a lot of love and that I had enough for both of us. She lay very still in bed while I told her how I had felt for her since we were both 14 years old. I talked about all the good times we had had in our almost 15 years of marriage. I told her how much our three kids meant to me and how secure I felt at home with my family.

The only reply was silence. I realized my marriage was over, and I cried.

The next day I wanted to eat one last meal together with my family. My belongings were all packed and loaded, and I was supposed to leave right after supper. I knew that I would have to tell my kids goodbye, but I didn't know how I would do it when the time came.

At the supper table everyone was quite solemn. None of us had a lot to say. I would get choked up; my eyes would water; my nose would run; and I couldn't talk. Finally I couldn't take it any longer, and I made my break for the door. I had made up my mind that my kids would not see me cry.

As I made my run for my pickup, my kids were in

close pursuit. And by now I was totally out of control. My children had now seen a grown man cry, and that man was their father. My oldest son, Allen, stood on the porch with his head hung down. My little girl, Susan, was on the sidewalk with her face in her hands. And my baby, Jay, was hanging on to the door handle of my pickup screaming, "Daddy, don't leave."

By then I couldn't say anything. I broke Jay's grip on the door and drove away. In my mirror, I could see him chasing me and then falling down. I knew that he was also crying because the best buddy he ever had had just left home.

My clothes were in the back of the pickup. My personal things like my shaver were in a green plastic trash bag on the floorboard. I felt like I was a piece of trash in that green plastic bag.

Earlier in the day, I had rented a two-bedroom apartment. Apartment living did not help matters any. In one day's time, I had changed from a safe, prominent neighborhood to a place full of strange people of different races and lifestyles. I thought I was better than they were because my situation was different. I was so busy thinking about getting mugged in the parking lot that I never gave any thought to the situations that may have put them there also.

I hated that apartment. I called it my arm pit. The only furniture I had was a blue couch which I had brought from home. This couch became my kitchen table, my bed, my desk. I didn't see any need for getting other furniture because I still felt that any day Nancy would see what she was doing to me, to herself and to our children. I thought she would call me back home and everything would be all right again. I lived with nothing but that blue couch for six months before I began to realize that Nancy wasn't going to change her mind.

After a while anger started to take over my life. When things wouldn't go right, I would get mad; and whoever was the closest got the brunt of my anger.

I was angry because I was single. I wished that Nancy had died so I could at least have been single with dignity. I was angry about the role I had to play as a *divorced* man.

I was angry at women. I was angry about lawyers and the court system. I thought that divorce lawyers were the parasites of the world.

Mostly I was angry at myself. I had let myself get in a position where I could get hurt so badly. I had never stopped work long enough to develop a hobby or to learn to play golf. I had never learned to cook, clean house or make a bed. I couldn't even take care of myself. I felt angry and helpless about all this.

The first time I did my wash was at the apartment laundromat. I had reached the point where I was either going to have to wash or move. The floor was literally covered with dirty clothes. It had been two months since I had left home, and I had already gone through my cleanest dirty clothes. I thought that if I went real early Sunday morning, no one would be there. It would be so obvious that a man alone doing his wash was a divorced man.

There was a woman there, about 40 years old. She

probably thought she would be the only one there, the same as me.

I had one box of soap powder for three loads of clothes. I figured that should be enough: a third of a box for each load. I tried to act as if the woman was not present, but I knew good and well that she was watching. I did everything like I was supposed to. First, the clothes in the proper order, no shorts and jeans together. Second, the proper amount of soap. And then, 35 cents to make it go. To my amazement, nothing happened. I calmly changed washers, gave it another shot of soap and another 35 cents. And still nothing.

After the third try I was whipped. I had no more soap. I was so angry I grabbed hold of the washing machine and was about to turn it over when my eye caught the lady who was surely also divorced. So I set the machine down straight and asked if she knew which machine worked. She said they all worked if you closed the lid.

I gathered up my clothes and told myself I would come back next week when it wasn't so crowded. I was angry with Nancy for forcing me into this kind of life that I hated so much.

I started drinking, and for over a year not one day went by without my getting drunk at least once. Sometimes an early start and then a nap would allow me to get in a double. This was the only way I could cope.

I had drunk very little in my first 33 years of life, but in that one year, I made up for a lot of lost time. I had also stopped working. I went home the night Nancy had called to say she was filing for divorce, and I never went back to finish the job. I didn't work for 15 months. I just couldn't make myself work.

The "simple, friendly divorce" didn't turn out to be so simple or friendly. The proceedings took six months, and at the end I was without my wife, my children, my home and my business. I was obligated to make large monthly payments and I had no way to meet them. Nancy's lawyer tried to prove I could pay a large alimony and child support. At the divorce hearing, there were four bankers and also people from whom I had contracted work who testified that I had made good money. As they took the stand, I watched with special interest because down deep I knew I would never work with them again. I was finished.

I don't like to talk about finances, but that became one of my biggest problems. My debts had accumulated to over $40,000. It would have been easy to declare bankruptcy, but I couldn't bring myself to do it. On top of everything else, I was humiliated to be around my family. I had borrowed a lot of money from my cousin and from my dad. Even though I had just about stopped caring about anyone or anything, I still cared enough to want to pay my debts someday. Especially to my family.

About this time, I got a police record. I had taken a dislike to Nancy's attorney and refused to pay my child support and alimony to him. I would rather pay her in person. For doing this, I was found in contempt of court and sentenced to 30 days in jail.

Then one of the banks where I owed money decided to close my checking account and put the money toward a note payment. At the time I had three checks out and so they were all returned marked "account closed." I was arrested for three counts of bogus checks. My only crime prior to this was a speeding ticket. Now I was a regular Al Capone.

I couldn't believe my life had changed so much. I felt like I had been turned inside out. Everything about me was the opposite of what it had been before my divorce. At that time I didn't know terms like *denial* and *depression.* I would just say I felt shitty!

Pal's Story

It was on a beautiful calm Monday morning, the Monday after Palm Sunday, that my life changed completely. From the west window in my husband's seventh floor hospital room, I could see our church, the church we both loved.

Just the day before—Palm Sunday morning—he had asked if there were many cars arriving for the beginning Holy Week service. He mentioned how appropriate it was for a very good friend to send him a lovely palm in its shining white pot. Palms for Palm Sunday!

And now, as if to turn our thoughts toward the victory of Holy Week, the resurrection, an Easter lily was being delivered by the pleasant little gray-haired lady who looked so crisp and prim in her clean pink uniform.

The doctor was making his rounds. We had heard his name on the intercom and were anxiously awaiting his visit. We wanted to be home for Easter and he was the one who, with a few magic words, could make it happen! After he examined Woody, he optimistically said, "You'll be going home in a few days."

Our daughter dropped by to say hello from the doorway. She was catching a cold so couldn't come in. She took me downstairs for a quick cup of coffee. When I returned to Woody's room, he was sitting on the side of the bed as he often did. We visited quietly for a while. He seemed so tired.

Then he asked me to stand behind him and rub his shoulders. I did. In a while his head dropped a bit and I asked if he was getting sleepy. I couldn't distinguish if he was nodding yes or if he was going to sleep. When his head dropped a bit more, I pulled him back in my arms. He looked at me and then slumped.

I screamed for a nurse but no one could hear. In my frenzy I called for Code Blue, and then ran to pull the cord for the unit. In what seemed hours to me, a nurse and the team came.

When they ushered me out of his room, I protested to the point of almost physically fighting with the nurse. "But I want to stay with him," I shouted. He had asked me to stay with him in the hospital and now—at this crucial time—they wouldn't let me be with him.

Within a few cruel moments, the love of my life, the person I loved most in this whole wide world, was gone and my life was being completely torn apart. God! Don't let this be happening. I cried uncontrollably for a few moments. Then the old trained reactions took over. I thought I needed to be in control of myself before my children got to the hospital.

My pastor sat with me while I repeatedly said, "I can't imagine living without Woody." The words I spoke were sad but controlled, unlike the pain inside my head which screamed, "It isn't true! It isn't true! Don't let this be happening."

The pastor got my oldest son, Scott, on the phone. I had coached myself to talk very slowly so I could keep from crying. And it worked. Scott was trying equally hard to believe and comprehend my carefully chosen words.

The next few days were nightmarish. I felt numb. I was so concerned that our son, Kent, wouldn't get home in time. He was in the Navy, en route to Hong Kong. I wanted all five children to be with me to help make decisions, but we had to plan the funeral without Kent.

It was Holy Week—and it would soon be Easter. Each lily that arrived at the house reminded me of those words, "Home for Easter." Yes, he was truly home for Easter.

My pastor assured me the service would be taped so Kent could hear it if he didn't get home. What wonderful people were at my side—four of my children, my oldest son's wife, my daughter's husband, my sister, the pastor and his wife, our many Church friends. I wanted them all around.

Yet I hardly remember what went on. I felt like a robot moving about mechanically, not caring if I made decisions or not. Woody and I had always made decisions together. Now I had to try to make all people understand my actions and my feelings. At times I wanted to scream and would bite my lips to keep from it. It was hard to keep my mask of control in place.

The second day after Woody's death, my brother-in-law asked me how much insurance we had. I don't know how or if I answered him. At that time I could not have cared less. Those things were very unimportant to me. Insurance, financial security—all the things Woody wanted me to have—I had *them* but I wanted Woody.

The day of the funeral I got up early; I went to be with Woody and wait for Kent. Two hours before the service, Kent arrived in his Navy uniform. He looked tall, handsome, tired, sad—and dirty, for he was wearing the clothes he had on when they notified him of Woody's death.

When the funeral was over and everyone had gone, the loneliness grew. Nights were the worst times. When I'd try to sleep, I would end up sitting straight up in bed, more wide awake than ever. I couldn't lie there. As soon as I'd lie down, I'd begin thinking about all the conversations Woody and I had had as we lay in this same bed, how we talked about our children, our home, our dreams for the future. Sleep just wouldn't come. I would plead with God to help me bear the excruciating pain, loneliness and heartache.

Many times I'd think, "If only the Code Blue Team had gotten there more quickly," and, "Why didn't we talk about death and dying more?"

The role and responsibility of being both father and mother to our youngest son terrified me. Each decision about the house or car seemed monumental. Should I have the leak under the kitchen sink fixed, or should I have new pipes put in? What plumber should I call? Would the plumber see that I was alone and cheat me? I lost confidence in myself.

Sue's Story

My marriage of 11 years ended in March of 1975. We had had a stormy year and had moved back to Oklahoma from Wisconsin to try to put our lives and our marriage back together—or so I thought.

We were staying at the home of Gary's parents with our four children. Things were not getting any better. The very air we breathed was charged with tension and unspoken anger.

Thinking a brief separation would help us both to see things more clearly, I decided to go to my brother's home in Houston for a couple of weeks. While there I read books which told me I was okay, I attended lectures on learning to cope, and I had long talks with my sister-in-law about dealing with marital problems. Toward the end of my visit, I was feeling very hopeful about our future together.

One evening I called Gary. I wanted to tell him that I knew there was hope for us. But I never got the chance. He assured me that he and the children were fine. Then he quietly announced that he had seen a lawyer and wanted a divorce. He was also seeking custody of the children because he felt I was incapable of raising them.

I was sitting on the floor in the upstairs hallway as those words came over the telephone wires. My head began to pound as I absorbed the meaning of his words. Images of our four children flashed before me: Mike, serious, shy, my first child; Tony, blonde, freckle-faced, always hungering for attention; Katy, our first girl, so sweet and sensitive; Carrie, the youngest, demanding, energetic.

I screamed into the phone, "You can't do this! You'll never get my children!! I'll fight you—and this time *I'll* win!" I slammed down the receiver.

The whole situation seemed unreal. Not 10 minutes earlier when I had dialed the number to reach Gary, I had been full of hope and anticipation. Now my world had crumbled. It just couldn't happen that quickly!

I thought I would explode until finally the tears came. They came in torrents. I cried out loud to God. "Please don't let this happen. I can't live without my children." I carried on until no more tears would come. Then I walked around in a daze. I just knew I was dreaming. This couldn't be happening to us. My sister-in-law gave me something to calm me down. I doubled the dosage and welcomed the darkness that enveloped me.

My first thought upon waking was to go back right away, to face Gary and to persuade him to give us another chance. I could change if that's what he wanted. God, I'd do anything! I prayed; I bargained; and I denied what I had heard.

When I arrived back in Oklahoma my husband came to pick me up and we rode home without a word. I was afraid to speak. I couldn't get any words past the lump of fear that was stuck in my throat. I was afraid to hear what he might say.

At the house, I learned from Gary's mother that, shortly after I had gone to Houston, Gary had brought his girlfriend from Wisconsin to be with him in Oklahoma.

This was more than I could stand. I confronted him. I flew into a rage and we began hurling insults, threats, even blows at each other. The scene was ended only when his mother stepped between us.

I knew I couldn't spend even one night in the same house with him. A friend offered me a place to stay and I moved out. All I had were my clothes. I had no idea how I could support myself and the children. But I knew I'd find a way. I told the children we would be together soon.

During those first few months, anger supplied me with the will and the energy to survive. I was determined to find a way to provide a home for my children. If I had stopped to think of the odds against me—no car, no money, no training—I might have given up. But I had to make it! I had to show him that I was somebody to be reckoned with! I told myself that the children and I were not only going to make it, but we would even be much better off without him.

It was slow going at first. The job I got was menial; the money not nearly enough to enable me to go off on my own. I worked in a cafeteria about three miles from where I was staying. I had no car. By the time I walked there, dished up food for 7 hours, and walked home, I felt like my legs would drop off. The ache in my body and in my heart almost defeated me. But I wouldn't give up.

To keep up my determination I kept feeding my anger, dwelling upon the humiliation, the hurt, the betrayal I had felt at the hands of this man I had vowed to love until death. After a couple of months, the court awarded me financial support. I got a better job and rented a house. At last, I could have my children with me again.

Once the children came to live with me, life began to settle into a routine. I thought life would get better. I didn't know it could get worse. The feelings of anger were now often replaced with fears of an unknown future and a subtle hopelessness that I couldn't shake. I was alone, and a black shroud of pain and misery was overwhelming me.

Depression began to swallow me up. Everyday chores became impossible hurdles. Standing in the kitchen fixing dinner seemed to be one of the worst times. I would stand there for minutes just looking at the potato or carrot in my hand. A great lump would rise in my throat and the tears would spill down my face. Sometimes I couldn't finish getting dinner ready.

I had never been very decisive. But at this point, I couldn't make *any* decisions. Decisions about where we would live, what schools the children should attend, sometimes even what I should buy at the grocery store: I couldn't see what difference any of it made. Let them decide. I just wanted out!

My thoughts kept coming back to one way that I could end all my pain: suicide. No matter what lay ahead for me in eternity, I thought it couldn't be any worse than the hell I was living here.

Many times I started to carry out these thoughts. I always waited until the children were gone for a few days. Then I would write notes, telling everyone why I had chosen this path and how sorry I was that I let them down. But I would end up throwing the notes away. I would remember the grief and guilt I had felt when my father ended his life. I knew I couldn't leave my children to go through what I had gone through.

I tried turning to God. I told him I was not strong enough to handle this. I begged him to show me what to do, how to cope. But he didn't seem to hear me. I couldn't bring myself to go to church. I was a divorced woman! I was unworthy. I began to feel like God was as far away from me as everyone else was. The sense of being completely alone overwhelmed me. I was dying inside.

My mother and sister were aware of my despair and they must have suspected my thoughts of suicide. They sought out a psychiatrist and tried to convince me that he would help me learn to cope.

In the beginning I hated each and every session. I would drive to his office in the brown '70 Oldsmobile my brother had given me and sit there in the car, smoking cigarettes, listening to the car radio, trying to get the courage to go in for my appointment. When the session was over I would go straight home and, although it was early in the morning when we met, I would go right to bed and draw the covers over my head. I wanted to block out his words in the darkness.

I used every means at my disposal to convince the doctor that my case wasn't worth his time. I even tried to flunk the ink blot test! Surely such an intelligent man could see he would get nowhere with me. But he was a persistent man. He kept asking me to return for just one more session, not to quit just yet. So I continued to see him, protesting all the while that it didn't make sense. I was worthless!

Reflections

Grief takes its own time, and it's always too long. One reason it is too long is that hurt people are reluctant to move into it. They hate to let go of the denial which begins the grief process because as soon as they let go of denial, they are face to face with their loss and the long journey through grief.

Gene didn't want to believe Blanche's death. So he cushioned it. First he prayed. He bargained. Maybe God could undo her death. If Gene would promise to be a better man, maybe God would let Blanche be alive. Even after Gene's call to the funeral home resulted in facts that pointed undeniably to Blanche's death, he recalled stories he had heard of mistaken identities.

By using these denial techniques, Gene gave himself an opportunity to absorb the reality of his loss over a period of several days instead of letting it hit him all at once.

Pal's denial of Woody's passing was more difficult to hang onto because she was present at the moment of his death. She had, however, denied the imminence of his death by saying he would be home for Easter. After Woody died, Pal masked much of her grief under the appearance of control for the sake of the children. But behind her calm words and composed face, denial still claimed some time. Inside her head, Pal's emotions screamed, "It isn't true. Don't let this be happening."

Earl's denial lasted much longer than Gene's or Pal's. At first he refused to listen to Nancy on the phone. Then he presented a well-planned bargain. He would reform. He would make her rich. He could love her enough for both of them.

When that didn't work and Earl moved away from home, he still denied his loss. He wouldn't get any furniture because this separation wasn't going to last.

In time, reality slipped between the chinks of Earl's denial. So he then chose the ancient denial technique of drunkenness. He could not bring himself to let go of denial and to face his loss and the long, slow road of grief.

Denial seems to linger longer in cases of divorce. Sue, like Earl, spent months in disbelief. Hers, however, began long *before* the divorce. She denied that her marriage was as shaky as it actually was. If she and Gary could move back to Oklahoma, they could work everything out. Through reading and conversation, she boned up on information about coping with marital stress. In these ways, she denied that the relationship was over.

When Gary announced his intention of divorce, Sue felt "unreal." She bargained. First, with God. Then she planned a bargain for Gary. She would change in whatever way he wanted her to change. The bargain didn't work.

Eventually, Gene, Pal, Earl and Sue let go of denial. Anger was waiting. In fact, anger had already slipped in without waiting for the final departure of denial.

In Earl's case, anger was both diffused and specific. He experienced diffused anger toward lawyers and women in general. Specifically, he turned anger against Nancy and against himself.

His anger against himself was most obvious. He took up habits that hurt only him. He quit work, let his debts accumulate, isolated himself from his family, and weakened his health by not eating properly and by drinking heavily. For Earl, anger was a particularly treacherous part of grief.

Sue's anger was specifically aimed at Gary. Whereas Earl's denial and anger left him debilitated, Sue's seemed to fuel her energy. She even "fed" her anger so she would have the energy and courage to go on against crushing odds.

Diffused anger is more typically experienced by widowed persons than by divorced persons. Pal had a momentary flash of anger toward the nurses who would't let her stay in the room while they tried to revive Woody. Although she quickly masked her anger, it was present along with denial in the words screaming in her head, "It isn't true!" But the anger, like the words, were left dangling. They weren't addressed to anyone in particular. Just to the situation. Pal's was a typical example of diffused anger.

Gene, in the bold tradition of the ancient psalmists, expressed his anger directly to God. "Well, I hope you're satisfied. It seems you've always got to deal out some misery when things are going well."

That could have been another verse to Psalm 22: "If the Lord likes you, why doesn't he help you?"

Words like these spring from such depths of the human heart and with such straightforward emotion that they are surely among the most perfect prayers. God understands anger. And he understands the faith that enables some people to speak that anger without camouflage.

For Gene and Pal, anger seemed to last for a shorter time than it did for Sue and Earl — at least their obvious and conscious anger. The anger that didn't get expressed became part of grief's depression. Gene experienced diffusion of anger in his short temper and edginess toward his children.

Just as each person expresses denial and anger in different ways, so does each person experience depression differently.

For Sue, depression came as anxiety, sleeplessness and indecisiveness. For Gene it came in edginess, temper flare-ups and discouragements. Nostalgia robbed Pal of sleep. Earl's depression seemed most severe. As he described it, he felt as if he'd been turned inside out. His behavior seemed to run counter to everything he had been before his loss. And the behavior intensified his depression.

Eventually Earl, Gene, Sue and Pal moved on to some degree of acceptance. They will describe their experiences of acceptance and new life in more detail in the following chapters.

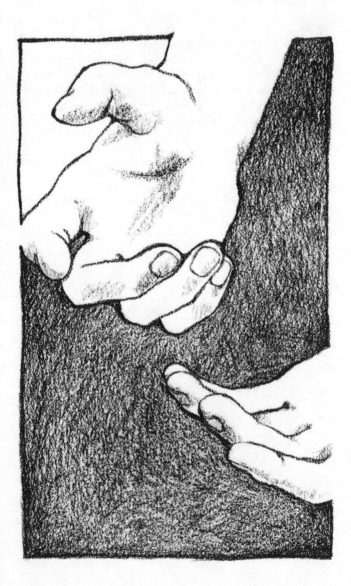

2. Restoring Damaged Trust

People are not loved because they are lovable, philosphers say. Rather people are lovable because they are loved. When people are loved, they feel worthwhile. They feel good. Special. Attractive.

When women and men lose a person who has loved them they are apt to feel unloved. And because they feel unloved, they feel unlovable. They feel bad. Worthless. Unattractive. In short, they lose trust in themselves.

Trust is not to be confused with confidence. Confidence says, "I can pass the test." Trust says, "I'm okay whether I pass the test or not." Confidence says, "I know I can depend on your loyalty." Trust says, "I know you love me — and I love you — even though you may have moments of disloyalty." Confidence relates to ability and habit. Trust relates to *being*.

Whether directed toward the self or toward others, trust involves esteem, acceptance, dependability and security. To lose trust is to lose an important element in life.

When a great loss rips through people's lives, it

damages their trust in three major areas: trust in self, in others and in God. For trust is all of a piece. It is difficult, for example, to have a profound trust in others without also believing in oneself. And it is almost impossible to trust God without believing that one is worthwhile simply because he loves us.

People's basic trust patterns are formed very early in life. For just as people can never see their own faces except in reflection, so they cannot get an objective view of the kind of persons they are except by the way others "mirror" them.

If, as children, people are ignored or put down by their parents or other significant persons, they perceive that they are not worth much. Since that is the way they are reflected, that is the image of themselves they begin building. If, on the other hand, they are smiled at, talked with, listened to and touched with affection, they perceive that they are special and worthwhile.

Although the basic trust stance *begins* in childhood, it is not irrevocably set then. All their lives people depend a great deal for their self-image on the way they are mirrored by other important people. Usually, after young persons leave home, the most important persons in their lives are their spouses.

By the way they respond to their spouses, husbands and wives mirror each other.

Spouses affect not only trust in self but also trust in others. When people's spouses love and affirm them they are inclined to think that the world surely holds many other good persons who can accept and love them. Since spouses so heavily influence people's basic trust, it stands to reason that when they lose their spouses, their trust is shattered. At least for a while. This diminishment of trust occurs whether they are widowed or divorced. In the case of divorce, however, the loss of trust may be accompanied with more bitterness and may be more difficult to regain.

Loss of trust is threefold.

First, hurt persons lose trust in themselves. After all, if they had been worthwhile, their spouses would not have left them. Maybe no one else can accept them either. Maybe they aren't acceptable. Even people who lose their spouse through death have this feeling of being "left." Reason may tell them that the death of the spouse was not a rejection, but the loss often *feels* like a rejection.

Second, they lose trust in others. These persons, their spouses, had vowed to love them and now they have left. Single-again persons begin to feel that it doesn't pay to trust anyone with their hearts. There is too much danger of being hurt again. They draw back. They may defend their withdrawal with fear or with bitterness. In fear they say, "My habits are set now. I don't think I could adjust to anyone else." In bitterness, they generalize: "Women are all selfish." "Men are beasts." "It doesn't pay to invest that much of myself in another person."

Third, they may lose trust in God. In the play *J.B.* by Archibald MacLeish, J.B. says, "If God is God, he is not good. If God is good, he is not God." That describes the way we often feel when we suffer a great loss. A *good* God would not let so much pain come. On the other hand, a God who is powerless to prevent the pain isn't much of a God!

For some people, this experience of losing trust in God seems either not to come at all or, if it does come, to last for only a short time. For others, these feelings last for months or for years.

When trust is damaged, where does the mending begin? It can begin wherever the damage is: in oneself, in others or in God.

For some people, trust begins to mend in the depths of their own psyches where their sense of personal worth has become firmly rooted. For, although their self-image depended initially on the way others saw them, in time these people come to believe in their own goodness regardless of whether someone else sees it or not. From this point of self-trust, they can rally and begin to trust others again.

In other instances, the mending of trust begins when others genuinely care for the hurt persons, listen to them, affirm them. It sometimes helps if these helpers know from their own experience how bewildering and painful the loss is. But the most important qualification is that the helping others are important to the grieving person and genuinely care. When caring persons are willing to give time and hearing, single-again people rediscover their worth.

A third mending point for torn trust can be found in a mature relationship with God. Mature. The difference between a mature and an infantile relationship with God depends on the way people view his activity in their lives.

Some see God as a kind of puppeteer who,

according to a prewritten script, pulls the strings of their lives, sets certain characters on stage, snatches others away and directly controls all their own entrances, exits and actions on stage. They have absolutely no choice in the way this little drama will be played.

People can react to this view of God's activity in their lives by shaking their firsts at him, by ignoring him or by giving up responsibility for the way their lives go. In the latter case, they say, "I turn it all over to you," and then sit back to see what strings he will pull. They piously figure that God will work it all out for them in the end.

It is easy to fool oneself into thinking that this kind of reaction is a mark of trust in God. But if it is, it is infantile trust. It is also poor theology. It denies one of God's first gifts to us: free will. Along with that denial, it sidesteps responsibility.

A more mature view lets people see themselves as God's adult sons and daughters who share in the responsibility for their own lives. God is their father and friend who walks beside them down whatever roads they travel. God neither wants them to suffer, nor will he take the suffering away.

This does not mean God is indifferent. It means that he trusts them and gives them freedom and responsibility. He may not take their pain away, but he helps them straighten their backs and walk through it. He helps mainly through his powerful presence. He gives gifts: life itself, good sense, feelings, freedom. He encourages grieving persons to use these gifts to reach out for what is good and true and beautiful.

Mature trust in God, then, does not reside in the belief that he will *take over* lives but that he *supports* people in their lives. He inspires them and strengthens them. Most importantly, *he* believes in *them*!

If God cherishes people so much, they must be worthwhile. They are worthwhile to God even if they have been guilty of great infidelities and injustices, even if they are confused or bitter, ugly, old or angry.

To paraphrase the philosophers: God does not love people because they, in themselves, are so irresistably lovable. No. People are lovable because he loves them. And they are lovable, too, because deep inside them, God has printed his own image and likeness. He sees his own image in them, and they can see it, too, if they will look.

The loss of trust people experience when they lose their spouses is real and awful. But it is not irremedial.

Pal's Story

I can still see my mother sitting at her quilting frame singing the beautiful hymns we all knew. My parents' faith in God and in their marriage was so evident that I learned to trust both my parents and God at an early age. I also trusted myself up to a point. However, I quickly learned that some feelings were not acceptable and when I had those feelings, I felt ashamed. I did not trust my parents to accept me with those feelings. One set of feelings that I couldn't trust myself to have was related to grief.

I grew up seeing and knowing death, and I learned very early that I was not to cry at funerals. Crying was a sign of weak faith! My grandmother died when I was 12 years old. I adored her. How my heart ached when she was gone!

In those days, we had the wakes in our homes instead of in funeral parlors. Seeing my grandmother there in the casket in our front room and knowing I could never talk to her again made me so sad. When I cried, my mother would say, "Don't cry. Be a good Christian. She lived a good life and now she's with God." This seemed to mean that if I cried, I wasn't a good Christian. I swallowed my tears back.

After the wake, we had the old-fashioned kind of funeral for my grandmother. I was a flower bearer. All of the flower bearers wore white dresses and walked in a procession. We had to be very composed. I honestly don't remember crying at the funeral. But I remember the ache.

That same ache was there when my younger sister died at one and a half years. I would not let myself cry. We were a family of five children, but only an older sister and I survived. So grief wasn't new to me, but trusting myself to feel it was. This inability to show feelings of grief was to affect my later life. But in general, I had a good sense of self esteem.

I spent my school years at a Christian Day School. Learning to expand my trust in myself and others was not difficult there because of some of my teachers. They, like my parents, helped me feel good about myself.

My deepest trust in myself and in someone else came when I met Woody. If a man like him loved me, I knew I was someone special. During our 33 years together, we faced many hardships and much illness. But we weathered these storms together and my trust in Woody and in myself seemed to grow with each crisis.

One of the biggest challenges to my trust in myself came when one of our sons seemed to be having problems growing up. We took him to a counselor. I felt that I had been a failure as a mother. I loved my son so much and tried so hard to help him. I kept wondering what I had done wrong. I was ashamed and almost frantic. Through all of this, Woody supported me. He loved our son, too, but he never questioned my judgment. In his eyes, I was not a failure as a mother.

When Woody became ill the last four years of his life, the grief that I had suppressed as a child made it difficult for me to talk to him about death without becoming emotionally upset.

Woody seemed to find it as hard to talk about death as I did. One time, when our pastor came to bring Woody communion, Woody said, "I'm not afraid to die but I'm just not ready yet." We never referred to that statement again.

Another time when we were talking about the business Woody had, I asked him who he would like me to contact "if anything happens." He gave me the name of an attorney, and we didn't discuss it any further. I deeply regret that I didn't trust myself more to talk to Woody about his death. We both knew it was coming. But that old pattern of denying grief, of not trusting myself with those feelings, would not allow me to share the feelings with Woody.

After Woody's death, I felt completely consumed with fear and lack of self-confidence. The one who had reinforced my faith in myself was gone. I felt frightened and very "single." Because I felt so alone and unsure of myself, my trust in others was also weakened. It took a great deal of patience from my friends before I was able to believe they really cared for *me*.

I remember a phone call from a friend shortly after Woody's death. Our husbands had been good friends. She knew I was still a partner in the business Woody had had, and she offered her husband's help. She told me that her husband could meet me for lunch if that was a more convenient time. This affirmation of her faith in me was a spark of life I needed at that time.

While adjusting to my life as sole decision-maker, I have also been encouraged and affirmed by my children. My son Mark lives with me. When I come home from the office, it's good to know that Mark will be coming in soon. We have a good rapport. He feels free to come and go and to lead his own life. He and my other children have helped enrich my trust not only in myself but also in them and in others.

Even though I now have more confidence in myself as a single person, I still feel a little frightened and uneasy when friends ask, "Are you going to remarry?"

At first, questions like this would make me feel hurt, angry and even disloyal. The very thought of developing friendships with men or of remarriage frightened me and also caused me to feel guilty.

Remarriage may come some day. But for now, I am not interested. My life is full, satisfying and worthwhile as a single person. I feel I am worthy of being loved and accepted. I want to enjoy friendships with both men and women.

My friends and family have given me love and understanding and patience as I have gone through the valleys and hills of despair. Their care has rekindled my trust in them and, finally, also in myself. Today I enjoy touching and hugging and kissing them and sharing my deepest feelings with them. These things affirm my sense of self-worth.

Earl's Story

One of the first things I tried to take up after my divorce was golf. For about a month I played three or four times a week. I can remember how aggravated and discouraged it made me feel. My concentration had become so weak that I often couldn't remember where I had hit my ball. When and if I could find it, I would stand over it and try to block out of my mind everything that was bothering me. I would take a deep breath and swing. Almost every time Nancy's face would flash before me just at the critical moment. I would go limp. The firm grip that I had had just a few seconds before would now turn to jelly.

The way I played golf was also the way I was handling my situation. I had lost my grip on life. I would go limp when anything crucial happened. The person I had trusted more than anyone else in the world had just told me she didn't want to be my wife any more. At that moment, I lost trust in myself. I also lost trust in others.

When I think of trust, I think of honesty and dependability. I would like to try to give examples of what these two words meant to me before and after my divorce.

Honesty was something I developed early. When I was around 11, I stole a 25-cent pair of ear plugs used for swimming. The following Saturday afternoon at confession, I told the priest what I had done. The old priest told me I would have to "steal them back" to the store and to hope I wouldn't get caught while doing so! My fear of getting caught taking them back was far greater than my fear of taking them to start with. When I had returned those ear plugs, I knew I would never steal again. I had learned a lesson in being honest. I carried that lesson into my marriage and my work.

I was honest in my marriage. Nancy and I didn't share a lot. She did her job and I did mine. But we didn't try to hide things from each other.

The small construction company that was mine was built on honesty. I did all my work through verbal agreement. People could trust me, and I trusted most of them.

When my divorce happened, I quickly unlearned honesty.

One night while drunk on Tequila, I cheated a plumbing contractor out of $1,200 in a game of pool. To my amazement, I didn't feel guilty about it! Instead I had a good feeling of revenge. I had been cheated in life, and now for the first time, I was the cheater. By using my divorce as an excuse, I was able to justify all my actions of dishonesty.

To me, trust also means dependability.

At one time in my life, I felt as if I was one of the most dependable persons anyone had ever met. If I told a person I would do something or be at a certain place at a certain time, that person could count on me. The feeling of being dependable was good. My wife and children were dependent on me, and it felt good to know I would never let them down.

But after my divorce, I soon realized that I had depended on their dependence on me! It seemed like all of a sudden, I wasn't a person any more. All I represented was a money machine. I could be moved out of my home, have my kids taken away from me, lose everything that I had worked for all my life, and I was supposed to continue with life as if nothing had happened or as if I didn't have any human feelings. I couldn't do it. No matter how hard I tried, I couldn't make myself go on. I knew my life had been shattered.

Nancy had called me a work-aholic and said that was a big part of the reason our marriage had fallen apart. With that big word ringing in my ears and the knowledge that the first part of it had cost me my marriage, I was determined not to work anymore. I went from one extreme to another and, by doing so, I became very undependable.

Time began to mean nothing to me. Where once I had been 10 minutes early for meetings, I was now almost always late; and some times I wouldn't even show up at all. What difference did it make? I had no one who cared for me and no one to depend on me any more.

I finally began to think I needed one of my children to be with me, to need and to love me. I did everything I could to persuade my oldest son, Allen, to come and live with me. I even went so far as to turn him against his mother. Finally, with the promise that every weekend would be full of something different we would do together, he left home at the age of 14 to share in my misery.

But I wasn't dependable any more. The good times that I had promised failed to come. I still refused to work. I wouldn't cook much, and the housework and laundry were always behind. The only thing that I did different was to get up at a certain time each morning to see that he left for school. I refused to quit drinking. And some nights I didn't come home at all. Allen began to fall into the same kind of pattern. He started skipping school and staying out, and his counselor called me every week. I was beginning to spend more time at school than Allen was.

Finally I returned to work. I thought that would solve everything. But it didn't. By that time, Allen seemed to be where I had been after my divorce. He had seen a man and a woman change in front of his own eyes. His world was shattered at the early age of 14. It seemed like he had lost trust in himself as well as in his own parents.

Allen now lives with his mother again. To this day, I think he doesn't trust her or me. I feel sorry for him and ashamed of myself for what I've done to make him feel the way he does. Looking at Allen, I see how badly children are affected by divorce.

When I became undependable, I couldn't trust myself and Allen couldn't trust me either. I also had trouble trusting God.

For some reason, when I was young, I thought God and the Church were practically one and the same. If I didn't have the Church, I didn't have God.

I grew up in a small town in New Mexico where the Catholic school was so small that we had three grades in the same room. That's where I learned about God and the Church.

I was a happy boy during those school years, and maybe a little mischievous. I remember one feeling so good that I have trouble describing it: the feeling I had after I went to confession.

Every Saturday afternoon shortly after two o'clock, I would get my little white missal, go to church, sit down front on the left just behind the candles and, for some reason, pay a nickle to light a dime candle. Then I would psych myself up by telling myself how bad I was, and open my little white missal to the pages of sins. There were about three pages of them.

By the time I would get through the list, I would see how terrible I had been. I had committed every sin that a child my age could commit—all the way down to dirty and unclean thoughts. I wasn't sure what that meant, but my aunt seemed always to be pregnant and my old dog, Sandy, was always having a new litter of pups. It just seemed to me I couldn't think of anything dirtier or more unclean than that.

I'd go into the confessional and say, "Forgive me, Father, for I have sinned. It's been one week since my last confession. I've done everything but steal." That was number 16 in my Children's Missal, and I had been broken of that sin ever since I returned the ear plugs. I can just imagine the old priest thinking, "Here's that Frawner kid again." I would accept my penance and would feel right proud of the amount of it, for I knew that Pat Johnson was the only one in school that could beat me in penance. I think he had a larger missal to choose from!

I would leave church feeling so good and clean that I felt there wasn't a holier person walking than this little ornery person here. I would be good the rest of the day and all Sunday morning. No shooting marbles for keeps and no giving anybody a whipping, no matter how much they needed one.

After I received Communion on Sunday, while walking back to my pew, I would have to bite my cheek and look down at my feet because I knew that if I looked up, I would burst into laughter just because I was so happy. And I was holy.

Even when I was older and in high school, these feelings stayed with me.

But as an adult, I had not let God enter my life. By marrying out of the Church, I was no longer a full member. I felt that I wasn't wanted. Nancy's religious background and her family's feelings would not allow us to have our marriage blessed by the Church. Since I thought of the Church and God as one, I felt I wasn't wanted by God either. I believed I was living in sin.

Lots of times during the first years of our marriage, I would wake up in the mornings and sometimes in the middle of the nights with a terrible sickening feeling, knowing good and well that I was going to burn in hell for eternity. But I would not divorce my wife so I could go to heaven. I decided I would try to get as much happiness as I could until the day I died. I decided I would try not to think of my Church or of God again.

After my divorce, I met some people who had a strong faith in God. They seemed to be able to adjust better than I was doing. I remembered how important God had once been in my own life. So I decided I needed more faith and that the best way to get it was to read the Bible. I was determined to read it from start to finish.

After about 600 pages, I quit. I didn't like the God I found in the Bible. To me, God is not mean. He doesn't kill small children and women for things their ancestors did. He does not kill grown men because they aren't circumcised. I didn't like the part about Moses. I thought he was about half crooked. I really wanted to find God in the Bible, and I feel bad about not being able to.

I no longer think that God and the Church are the same thing. I go to Church off and on now, and sometimes I take my kids. There are some things I still don't like about Church, but I like the feeling that I get when I go.

My faith in God may be a little different from the faith others have, but my belief in God is profound. I believe that God is good. God smiles. He is kind. God didn't make me sad. He wants me to be happy. He gave me the good sense to know right from wrong. And the best helping hand he gives me is the one at the end of my own arm. God is my friend. A good friend of mine has helped me believe that there is a little bit of God in everybody. I look around at people and think of their goodness. When I see goodness in people—and in myself—it helps confirm my belief that God lives right here.

Trust in myself has also slowly been rebuilding. My feeling of being dependable again started when I went back to work. I had quit for so long, I didn't know if I could go back or not.

For the first two or three months after I started back, I did well just to show up. Before, I had been able to really take command of my work. Now I found I was uncertain about a lot of decisions I had to make. My works consists of drilling holes under highways for utility lines. By drilling underneath, there is no interruption of traffic. On the job I contracted for when I started working again, there were 16 crossings. The last one was under Interstate 40. I dreaded that one.

I had drilled the Interstate five years earlier just 500 feet from where this new crossing was to be. I remembered the trouble I had had then. In that particular area, the ground is sandrock, one of the hardest materials to drill. Taking into consideration the hardness of the ground, the length of the crossing and the large diameter of pipe we were using, the State Department had agreed to let me drill each lane separately. That meant I could take my equipment out into the center of the Interstate and, in that way, I could drill one-half the length of the hole at a time.

But now the State Department refused to let us work in the center. We would have to go 240 feet with one bore! That would have discouraged me five years ago! And now, still not feeling very dependable, I wasn't sure I could even attempt it. Deep down I knew that I still had not made a full effort to prove myself.

I remember standing in the office listening to the men I had contracted the work from. They were very upset with the State's decision not to let us work the center. They said the job was impossible. As I listened to them, I began to feel some of my former energy and I said, "If it can be done, I can do it." I knew that if I could get across, I would once again trust me. And just as important to me was the fact that others could also trust me.

I worked 16 hours a day for 14 days, and at four o'clock one sunny afternoon, I saw my trust come out on the north side of Interstate 40. I had done what they said was impossible.

My work is very important to me, and knowing now that I can do it has helped me rebuild trust in myself. I know I'm dependable again. I will continue to be a good man. I will never cheat another man as long as I live.

I would like my son, Allen, to know that nothing in life is permanent and that a shattered world can be put back together. And I trust that someday he can again trust me.

Gene's Story

In my youth, the trust I had in my parents was trust that they would always be there, provide for my needs and do all the things that would be beneficial for me. They never let me down.

The trust relationship I had with several of my close friends as I got older was at a different level. I was able to share my feelings, thoughts and convictions to a greater extent with them than I could with my parents. These friends never betrayed my trust.

The God I had known since I could first comprehend was also trustworthy at still another level. I knew from the earliest teachings of my parents and from the teachers at the Catholic schools I attended that God was all loving. For a half century I had no reason to question it, for during that much of my life, my trust in God had never really been tested.

And the trust that existed in my marriage? It became a special, unshakable bond between Blanche and me that was unspoken and ever present. From the time I first got to know Blanche well, I could feel a uniqueness in our relationship. We risked sharing our feelings with each other, and the way in which these feelings were received led to a lifetime of trusting and love. The years of our living together intensified our bond of trust.

When I first fell in love with Blanche, there was no mistaking the feeling, even though it was a new experience for me. I had told her how I felt, but my heart was so full that I wanted to let her know of my love in some special way. One time I decided to write her a poem. Why I settled on this idea, I don't know; for I certainly had no experience at writing poetry. But just the same, I wrote one. I put into that poem as best I could my feelings of love for her, what she meant to me, and how lasting I wanted our love to be.

Believe me, I thought a long time before I gave the poem to her, but one evening I did. The moment it was in her hand, I risked my entire future with her. And my children don't even know about this, but I risked them, too! For if Blanche had made light of that poem, or made it clear that my feelings didn't matter that much to her, most likely our relationship would have begun to fade away right then. As it was, I had really trusted her with my heart full of feelings, and she accepted it completely. She told me she thought my poem was beautiful and, with tears in her eyes, she proclaimed it to be one of her treasures. From that night on, my trust in her and in our relationship never wavered.

Having her love fulfilled me. It made me feel good about myself. It gave me confidence to dive headlong with her into our future. In marriage, our trust deepened. Trust was there when we bought our home; when each daughter was born; when Colette, our eldest, married; and when we buried our parents. At the end of 25 years together, we had reached the ultimate in our trusting.

I realize now that my trust was too narrowly directed. I did not risk trusting others on a level anywhere close to this one that was so special to me. I really didn't mistrust; I just didn't feel the need to experience trust outside the tight little circle where I could safely trust with no risk.

In looking back, 25 years did not seem like a very long time. It seemed incredibly short, in fact, when I realized that the one with whom I had intimately shared those years, those events, those feelings was gone. The one who knew me completely could know me no more. The one who could make me feel so good with just a glance, who could make my life so comfortable or be so reassuring when things didn't go right. Gone!

All of a sudden, I was basically alone. No opportunity to get used to the idea gradually, either. My comfortable life had flipped upside down in one minute, and I had never seen this side of life before!

I found myself in the unfamiliar role of a single parent with Kathleen and Lori, my teenage daughters, still at home. I found that all the things Blanche could do so easily were stumbling blocks to me. Cooking meals, shopping for groceries, doing laundry, making doctor appointments and doing the other million and one things that are required to run a home—all these in addition to my full-time job.

Like what did I know about bringing two teenage daughters to a wholesome maturity alone? Or helping them emotionally through the loss of their mother when I couldn't cope with it myself?

What was the secret of threading the sewing machine? Blanche could do it with her eyes shut! Or what did I know about suggesting which blouse to wear with that skirt? Why did the meatloaf turn out so terrible when we followed the recipe exactly? Or why was it so difficult for me to braid pigtails in hair as fine as silk? I'm still trying to find ways to make a large box of Kotex less conspicuous in the grocery cart and to look unembarrassed when the checker waves it around in the air searching for the price!

The demands on me left so little time for myself that I sometimes felt like I was on a rapidly moving treadmill going nowhere fast.

I felt defeated before I ever began. I didn't trust myself that much now and, because of the slipping trust, I found it harder to trust others. I misinterpreted sincere offers of help from caring people as "feeling sorry for me"; and I didn't want anyone to pity me.

I really wanted to ask favors of some, but I didn't trust myself or them enough to risk asking for their help. For example, I was faced with the immediate problems of getting Kathleen and Lori to and from school each day — something I could not accomplish myself because of my job requirements. And I needed someone to look after things at home while I had to leave town on business. But I was reluctant to ask anyone to help. I didn't know how it was going to work out, but I knew it was up to me to solve the problems alone.

I even began mistrusting some single-again women who seemed to be showing me some extra attention. One lady in particular, a widow whom I knew only casually, sent me thoughtful cards and phoned me occasionally. I misinterpreted her concern as an effort to gain my attention, and I wasted no time in putting up barriers to such approaches.

For a short time, I felt that the God I had loved and trusted had really let me down. Hard! I had always tried to let him know that I loved him. I tried to be a good father and husband. I had sacrificed so that my children could get a good Christian education. We had tried to make religion a part of our family life. He should have been aware of all that, but how does he repay? By taking from me the one person I loved most of all, that's how! And piling on burdens that I had never faced before. It just didn't make any sense to me. What good did her death do?

Father John was a man I trusted. I had known him a little more than a year, and Blanche and I had become close to him. He showed a maturity well beyond his 28 years; and when he spoke his feelings or convictions, his eyes and voice carried a sincerity straight from his heart.

That last Sunday before she died, John had touched Blanche's heart strings when he told her after Mass that she looked very pretty in her new outfit and that she had stood out to him from all the others each time he glanced out at the congregation.

Just five days later, he brought me the news of her

death. Even in my shock, I was touched by his caring and feelings. That night in my home, we were two men with a great loss affecting us each in our own way. I will never forget his willingness to accept so much of my burden. He stayed with me for over three hours then. In his way, he was hurting as much as I was.

Father John conducted one of the services for Blanche. With a lump in his throat and watery eyes, he spoke to the congregation — and I felt he was speaking directly to me — of God's limitless love, unchanging and pouring forth for us to accept or reject.

During that homily, I realized that God understands me better than I do myself and that he is big enough to handle my reactions of distrust. I began to understand that his love doesn't come and go, depending on how I accept it. I had the feeling that Blanche was experiencing this reality of God's love first-hand right at that moment, and that she now understood the mysteries that we sometimes talked about but which always before had left us wondering.

My lashing out at the God I loved had been a reaction from frustration, and I knew my love for him was firmly seated. Instead of feeling I had been short-changed in life, I began to realize that I had been greatly blessed by him. I was thankful that he had allowed us to have those 25 good years together, and all the goodness they produced: our five lovely daughters, the comfortableness of our relationship, the warmth of our love. Most of all, he had given me the faith to believe and trust in him.

And that is what I truly wanted to do. My trust in God was intact.

Trust in myself came back slowly. Although my life was different now, a lot of the old familiar remained. My home was exactly the same. So were my job and outside obligations. I had the same neighbors, the same friends, the same Church. My daughters were just as present as they had been before. I had struggled through troubles before, but the big difference this time was the huge hole in my life that I had to live with.

As trust returned, I allowed others to help me. I knew they wanted to do so because they cared for me, and nothing more. Our friend, Charlene, did not wait to be asked; she informed me that she was going to see to it that my girls had a ride to school. And, at considerable trouble to herself and her children, she kept her word.

Ruth, Blanche's co-worker and long-time friend, did much more than just "stand by" as I had asked her to do while I was on my business trips. She spent several nights at my home with my two daughters, keeping them company and treating them like royalty. They needed that companionship and it was a great comfort to me to know that they were in such good hands.

I learned that the lady who had seemed to come on so strongly was only relating to the pain I was experiencing and was just trying to comfort me because she knew and cared.

When I saw people caring like this, I began to cope better myself. Little by little I learned some of the basic rudiments of cooking and discovered how many ways a can of cream of mushroom soup can be used. We don't eat as elegantly as we did before, but so far none of us has lost any weight or gotten food poisoning. The laundry gets done, and the occasional wrinkled shirt doesn't seem as important now.

I have had to let some things slide that I wouldn't have considered allowing before. My garden is one example. As I look at the weeds that engulf the tomato vines, or see the paint that is peeling off the outside of my house, I make no apologies, for my priorities have changed. Relationships have become more important to me than upkeep.

I have become more concerned with family responsibilities, for I realize the need for my time and care there has increased considerably. I also identify much more now with the pain of loss and the emotional trauma that comes with the loss of a spouse through death or divorce, so I have become involved in programs that are structured to support those who are suffering such loss. There is a tremendous opportunity for peer ministry here, and just by taking the time to show that I care, I can touch someone and we both can come closer to the wholeness we crave. It's okay if I have to let the weeds grow in the garden while I listen to someone on the phone.

I find that I don't predict the future anymore. Practically all my adulthood was spent in a union with Blanche. To have that union shattered without hope of revival makes me wonder, at this point in my life, if I would be afraid or unwilling to risk that much again.

If I had had any choice, I certainly would not have considered the life-style I'm living now; but because I am single again, I am aware that my trust of others and of God has deepened and become richer. From the deep undertow of distrust, I have made it into the shallows of trust, and I hope that the solid footing of confidence lies just ahead. It has been a tough experience, but I have made the turn back, and I feel like I'm a better man because of it.

Sue's Story

I don't know where I got the idea I was bad. I just know it has been with me since my earliest days. Even as a child, I felt worthless and very lonely.

My best friend during my days as a child was Penny. She was a small white dog. We were inseparable. I can still remember how we would sit together on the front porch steps of our house in Tulsa.

Quite often I would feel lonely or unhappy with myself, and Penny always seemed to sense these moods. She would put her head in my lap and listen quietly while I talked. I never felt the need to hide my tears from Penny. When I would begin to cry, she would wag her tail slightly and gently lick my tears away. I knew she loved me.

I trusted Penny. I felt there was no one else who could listen to how bad I felt about myself and accept my feelings without rejecting me.

Trust in my family was limited to dependence on

them. I knew my parents would provide me with the basics—shelter, food and an education. But I did not trust that they approved of me.

Because of my bad self-image, I was constantly seeking approval from the important people in my life. I felt loved only as long as I was living up to their expectations.

Even in the smallest things, such as picking out a new dress, I deferred to my mother's judgment. I always chose the dress she preferred, even if I couldn't stand it. That way I was certain that my "choice" would meet with approval. I applied this behavior to everything I did. Even so, I seldom felt approved. And when I did, I knew that the next day I'd have to win approval all over again. I never simply felt that I *had* acceptance and love; I was always trying to *earn* it.

My feelings about God didn't do much to help me grow in trust. To me, God was my creator and my judge. He handed down a list of dos and don'ts for me to follow. He even gave me an example—his own Son. I understood that I was to be perfect, as he was. Since I wasn't perfect, I must be bad.

I attended Mass a couple of times a week with my class and again with my family on Sunday. Each time I went, the crucifix was the focal point of my attention. At Communion time, I would kneel on the cold white marble awaiting the host. My eyes were always drawn to the figure hanging behind the altar. I knew *I* helped put him there in that agony. How could he love me when I had caused him so much pain?

By the time I graduated from high school, I had

reinforced the patterns of my childhood. These patterns camouflaged my lack of trust in myself and in others. I thought I knew how to be accepted. I could find out what other people expected of me and do it. As for God, I tried to follow his rules to atone for my guilt. Religion was more of a burden then than a joy to me.

I met Gary during the first semester of my freshman year at college. Although I had received a scholarship and everyone was proud of my academic success, I was very unsure of myself in this strange new environment. I felt out of place on a big campus, and I was searching for someone to help me fit into the college scene. Gary became that someone.

As our relationship deepened and Gary began to profess his love for me, I felt it was important to let him know how I felt about myself. I knew my feelings of worthlessness were not typical, and I wanted him to know what kind of person I was.

I couldn't say the words, so I wrote him a letter filled with my feelings of self-doubt, my fears of disappointing him. I knew I was taking a big risk in exposing this part of me. What if he laughed at me? Or turned and walked away? But I had to know if he cared enough to listen and accept me as I was. I needed to trust him.

The night I gave him that letter we had been over at the Student Union with friends. On the long walk back to my dormitory, I was working up my courage. It was almost curfew, but I asked him if we could sit at the fountain in front of the dorm for a few minutes before I went in.

As I handed him the letter, my heart was pounding rapidly and my hands shook. He had to squint to catch the words in the light from the street lamp. My eyes filled with tears as I watched him read. How I loved him and wanted to be right for him. I was so afraid he wouldn't want me when he knew how insecure I was.

When he finished reading, he looked at me and said that he didn't understand all that I had said but that he loved me. I was so overwhelmed with relief and joy at hearing him say he loved me that I completely missed the first part of his answer. I had found someone who could love and accept me!

After we married, I wanted both my faith in Gary and his faith in me to grow. However, with the passing of each year, we seemed to talk less instead of more. We constantly moved from one state to another. Babies, lack of money, the demands made on him by his work: all these things seemed to get in the way when we tried to relate to each other on a deep level.

I wanted to recapture the feelings of joy and trust I had that night he read my letter. I wanted him to know me. However, when I tried to share my feelings with him, he began to back away. I seemed to be smothering him with my dependence. His answer the night he had read my letter came back to haunt me. He really didn't understand. Maybe he couldn't. That lack of understanding seemed to kill his love for me. My old feelings of self-doubt became stronger than ever.

Shortly before we left Wisconsin I learned of Gary's involvement with another woman. Gary and

I had not been close for some time, but I was not prepared for this. I felt rejection, humiliation and panic. The last shred of trust in myself was gone. If he were to leave, I would have nothing left. So when he assured me that he had no intention of divorcing me, I clung to that promise with everything I had.

Then, in March of 1975, my worst fears became reality. Gary told me he wanted out. My last bit of faith in him was shattered. The one person I had believed in, the only one I had really trusted to care for me, had set me adrift.

Who was left to trust? I couldn't ask God to come to my rescue. He had given me the grace to succeed in my marriage, and I had failed. I had never been any good, and this proved it!

I began to act out my sense of worthlessness by drinking and running around.

For a long time, I didn't talk to anyone about my despair. But after a while I knew I had to talk. At first I talked only to my psychiatrist. As my trust in him grew, I felt the need to trust and talk to others who were my peers.

The first person I reached out to was my sister, Joan. She had moved to Oklahoma City during my divorce proceedings. I could see in her eyes how much she longed to see my wounded spirit healed. We would sit at the counter in her kitchen and talk and talk. Although Joan had not experienced the agony of divorce, the way she listened and empathized with my pain was a source of strength to me. I could tell that her love for me was real. She didn't see me as a bad person. I began to search for the goodness she saw in me.

About this time I met a woman who, along with Joan, became my true friend. Judith listened to my story with acceptance and a gentle caring that allowed me to reach deeply into myself without judgment and to express not only the events of my life but also my feelings about them.

One day I went to the Family Life Office where Judith worked. I was feeling deeply troubled. My children were with Gary. I was unbearably lonely. I felt distant from God. And the old feeling of being bad was stronger than ever. When I got to Judith's office, I felt life humming. Phones rang, the secretary typed, people smiled as they came and went. It was like they were all living in a different world from my world. I couldn't identify with that life.

Judith greeted me and seemed to sense that something was wrong. We went into her private office. Then she pulled her chair up and sat facing me. We talked a while and then she asked me if I would like to pray.

As I prayed, the dam burst. Words tumbled out. I cried as I pleaded with God to help me see that I had a purpose, that I was not totally responsible for the pain I saw in my children's eyes. I told him of the despair and despondency within me. I asked his forgiveness for not being the person he wanted me to be. Then Judith prayed that I would begin to realize the power of God's love in my life. She prayed that I might accept myself and let go of all the bad feelings that kept me from feeling close to God.

I left Judith's office thinking there must be some good in me. I think I took a small step that day toward building trust.

Gradually during that year, I began to see God as someone I could trust. I had always had a relationship with him, but it had been built on guilt and fear. Now I saw a loving Father who knew my weaknesses and longed only for me to let him pick me up. He loved me because I was his daughter, Sue.

It took 32 years for me to begin to form a real, personal friendship with God. I still struggle with myself, but now I am able to talk with him as with my best friend. Each time I stumble, I feel him urge me to give life one more try. The knowledge that he is with me gives me strength.

The growth of trust in my life has been a guarded process. I am still lacking in a great measure of self-trust. I have learned a great deal about myself these past three years. I have always had a vivid view of my limitations and shortcomings. Now I am searching for a realistic acceptance of the goodness in me.

My trust in people like Joan and Judith, and my new trust in God, has made me more willing to open up to others. Now I can share some of my feelings with my mother without fear of rejection. I love her and I want her to know me. I am more open with my children. I try to let them see me as a person, not just as their mother. I hope that they will trust me enough to take the risk of sharing themselves with me when they need to turn to someone.

Reflections

When Earl drove away from his home after his last meal with his family, he noticed on the floorboard of his pickup truck the green plastic trash bag which held all his personal items. That trash bag became a symbol of the way he saw himself. He was like some disposable item that is used and then thrown out. Like a styrofoam cup. Or last Sunday's newspaper. It's difficult to believe in one's worthwhileness with that kind of image.

We are speaking of trust.

Economically speaking, Gene grew up in a middle-class family, Earl in a poor family, Sue and Pal in upper middle-class families. All four of them knew that their parents would feed and clothe them and send them to school. As a matter of fact, all four of them spent at least some years in schools that required special tuition payments. They knew they were worth feeding, clothing, educating and sacrificing for.

The growth of trust largely depended on early experiences of acceptance and esteem.

Even as a child, Sue showed some serious weakness in her trust. She did not feel good about herself and she didn't think anyone else could feel good about her. Since she didn't think people could accept *her*, she hoped they would accept her behavior. Life early became a relentless parade of approval-winning behavior.

The deepest kind of trust comes when we feel absolutely known and unshakably loved. Most of us do not experience such trust in an abiding way.

Gene is probably one of the exceptions. He had balked at sharing his feelings with his family. He had shared somewhat more with friends as a young man. But in marriage, Blanche became his best friend and his only confidante. At that time, Gene was not as self-reflective as he now is; but to the extent that he knew himself, he shared himself with Blanche.

Sue had a brief taste of this kind of trust the night she gave Gary her letter and felt understood and loved.

Earl, although he seemed to have that kind of trust in himself, did not expect it in his marriage. He simply expected the marriage to endure marked by basic acceptance and simple esteem.

Pal's trust bordered on this deepest level. But the off-limits feelings she had learned as a child remained off-limits in her marriage. At the very time she would have liked to enter consciously and deeply with Woody into the grief of his dying, the old pattern got in her way and denied them that experience of final intimacy.

Then these four marriages ended. What happened to trust in self and in others?

After Blanche's death, Gene began to realize that making her his only real confidante left him more alone than ever. By comparison, his other relationships were shallow. He also began to discover new things about himself: new sympathies, broader tolerances, different understandings of God and of the Church, whole realms of feeling he either had not experienced or had not reflected on before. And who was there to tell? He had trusted only one person and she was gone. Would he be willing to share that much again? Would anyone else be willing to receive that much of him?

Sue's divorce almost tolled the death knell of what little trust she had. She had less trust to lose, therefore her loss was greater. Initially, the only thing that kept her from feeling completely "disposable" and from acting on that feeling was her care for her children.

Both Sue and Earl felt like trash, and both behaved for a time according to that feeling. Their behavior reinforced their own poor self-image. It "proved" that they were unlovable. Trust was not only weakened; it was beaten into the ground. Sue's and Earl's reactions are typical. Many divorced persons go through a period of self-loathing. And many of them move their distrust beyond themselves to include others.

For Sue and Earl, learning to trust again came partly as a result of the acceptance and esteem that significant others had for them. In Earl's case, the sturdy self-trust he had developed as a child came to his rescue. In Sue's case, the rebirth of a trust that was already weak seems just short of miraculous.

In the restoration of trust, the need to be needed figured in all four stories. More specifically, the need to be needed by one's own children. Gene had daughters at home who required sensitive parenting. Earl, always a strong father, felt his fatherhood more acutely than ever. He had a message for his children and tried to find a way to give that message from a distance. Three of Sue's children were pre-school age at the time of her divorce. They were confused, hurt and angry; they needed her more than ever. Although Pal's children were older, one son still lived at home. And because of the closeness of the family, they needed one another.

And what of the future? Perhaps the final test of trust in others after the loss of a spouse is the ability and willingness to enter into an intimate relationship with commitment. This is not to say that single-again people ought to remarry or that they don't trust others unless they do. But deep trust leads people to reveal themselves intimately in loyalty and love.

Gene is aware of his desire for intimacy and of his fear of entering into marriage again. He is learning, however, to reflect on his feelings and to express them. He knows more about himself than he has ever known before, and he esteems himself. If he does remarry, he will bring a more self-reflective and complex Gene to the marriage. He will want his wife to be his best friend. But whether he remarries or not, he wants to continue developing close friendships.

Like Gene, Earl has become much more aware of his feelings and much more sensitive to the pain of others. He is developing deep friendships with both men and women. In future friendships, he will seek profound sharing and mutual esteem and acceptance. If he remarries, he will not again settle for a durable-but-surface relationship.

Sue is proving to herself that she is a good woman and a strong one. In future friendships, she will not be as dependent as she was in her relationship with Gary.

Pal is experiencing her individuality in a way that is personally fulfilling. The idea of remarriage is remote.

These four stories are unfinished because they are still being lived out. But even in their unfinished state, they make two important points regarding trust.

One point is that there is no predictable pattern in regaining trust. Unpredictability seems more predominant in cases of divorce than in cases of death. Who would have thought that Earl would have been so devastated for so long? Who would have dreamed Sue could rally?

The other—and more hopeful—point is this: Often the very grief that demolishes our trust also returns it to us enriched. All four of these persons are growing in a *quality* of trust that far surpasses their former trust. They are moving steadily toward that level of trust in which they know themselves thoroughly and can say, "I'm worthwhile."

This new life is a kind of resurrection. Not resurrection in history or in a book, but in life. God doesn't live in neat abstractions; he lives powerfully in the lives of his hurt and hurting—and hoping— sons and daughters. One way the power of his life in them is evident is in their renewed trust.

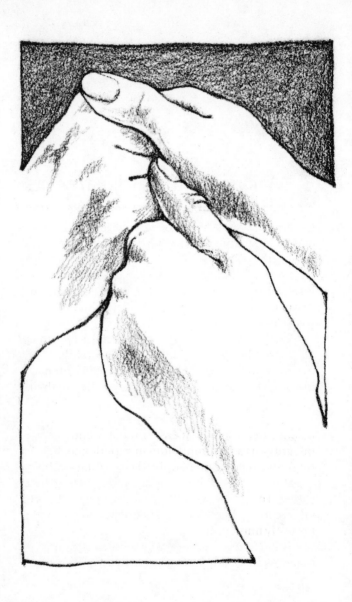

3. Making Sexual Adjustments

Conflict between sexual needs and moral values is almost inevitable when a marriage ends. Needs and desires do not diminish just because the circumstances of people's lives have changed. Physical and emotional needs are not part of their marriages; they are part of their very humanity. And so the needs endure.

Sexual needs are not the only needs people have. They also have a need for integrity. Sexuality demands that people live in some kind of intimacy; integrity demands that they live according to their values.

The very attempt to arrive at some kind of balance of these two needs—intimacy and integrity—is a profound human experience. It requires single-again people to face squarely their situation, to admit their feelings and to clarify their values. To wrestle with these God-given needs is to engage in the high drama of becoming more honestly human.

It is sad that so many people who witness this drama sit in judgment instead of in awe. They too often see weakness whereas, if they looked with compassion, they might see real courage. Perhaps only people who have suffered great loss and have confronted their feelings and sorted out their values—perhaps only these people can appreciate the *full* meaning of sexuality and integrity.

Sexuality is more encompassing than genitality. Sexuality includes genitality because it includes *every* human experience that moves people to give life to another person. People give and receive through care and concern, tenderness and affection, understanding and sharing. These qualities bring persons into intimacy with others.

Intimacy is sexual because it gives life. The life it gives may be emotional or physical. Or both.

There are degrees of intimacy. Physically, for example, one may be close to another by holding hands, by embracing, by caressing, or by having sexual intercourse. Emotionally one may draw close to another by sharing ideas, by revealing personal feelings, or by entering into deep friendship with another person.

Different people and different circumstances call for different degrees and expressions of intimacy. With one person, for instance, someone might share secrets in friendship. That would be an emotional intimacy that is life-giving. With the same friend, the expression of physical closeness might go no farther than a greeting hug. Both the friendship and the hug are sexual because they both express the need to give and to receive life.

Intimacy is most satisfactory when the emotional and physical expressions are congruent. Having sexual intercourse with a person one does not like is not congruent. It doesn't "match." It frustrates the need to be honestly life-giving in relationship.

In marriage, people try to bring the whole range of their sexuality to full expression. Ideally they have a profound emotional intimacy and, at the same time, they also have a full range of physical intimacy. Thus, when their marriage ends, loneliness is as much a part of their sexual loss as is the physical/genital ache. In both areas, they experience loss of intimacy.

Nevertheless, the loss of physical closeness seems to be most acutely felt. Perhaps one reason people who lose a spouse are inclined to center the whole burden of loss in the area of physical frustration is that total physical intimacy is a *special* mark of marriage. Even though friendship is part of a good marriage, it is not exclusive to marriage. People can experience friendship before and outside of marriage. Regular physical intercourse, however, is most commonly and legitimately experienced within marriage. Sexual intercourse, therefore, becomes the primary symbol of all that has been lost.

Perhaps it is because sexual intercourse is so closely bound to marriage that single-again people feel their sexual loss most acutely in physical frustration. In fact, they sometimes feel that if they can satisfy *that* need, they will be sexually satisfied. The fact is, however, that while they may be physically satisfied, they may not be sexually satisfied. They forget that their sexual loss is a loss of intimacy in *all* areas.

In the case of divorce, there may be another reason for concentration on feelings of physical frustration. For in divorce, real loss of intimacy—full intimacy—comes long before the divorce is finalized in court. Even in cases where a couple is genitally active up to the legal end of the marriage, intercourse is not life-giving for them in an emotional way. In other words, the physical closeness and emotional distance becomes an experience of sexual incongruency. Sensitive persons nearly always feel profoundly rejected in these situations.

Since rejection is hard to take and since physical intercourse is the predominant symbol of intimacy and acceptance, divorced persons often try to reexperience acceptance and a feeling that they are worthwhile by engaging in sexual activity. This tendency perhaps explains why such a high percentage of divorced persons are "sexually active."

Trying to restore self-esteem and acceptance through physical intimacy does not usually work. Very often, divorced persons simply reenact the sexual incongruency they experienced in marriage. If they, for example, had physical closeness without emotional closeness, they are apt to repeat that pattern in casual sexual relationships. In marriage they missed friendship, so they withhold friendship from their other sexual partners. Actually this behavior can be a kind of revenge. A sexual partner can become a substitute for the former wife or husband. This kind of behavior stems from some blind, irrational impulse to "do unto others as someone has done unto me."

Widowed persons do not as frequently suffer these feelings of incongruency in their marriages. They do not often experience the same sense of personal rejection. Loss, yes; but not rejection of their most private selves. It is not surprising, then, that statistical studies indicate that widowed persons are less apt to enter into casual physical intimacy than divorced persons are.

But widowed persons often reenact their loss in another way. Their sexual partner left them absolutely. Their departure is permanent. So the widowed person may absolutely cut off any chance to reenter any intimate relationship. One way of doing this is to idealize the former spouse in such a way that no living person could ever match up. This idealization scares people away—and so the widowed person is left absolutely single.

Besides physical frustration, confusion of values is another problem that nearly always attends the loss of a spouse.

The values people hold form a kind of network. When one part of that network is gone, all the other parts shift. When values are in this shifting or adjusting process, people may seem to have thrown overboard all that they once lived by.

Some people refer to this period as "the crazies." But actually, the grieving persons are simply readjusting, clarifying and deepening their values. They are seeking integrity, or balance, between their needs and their values. And that is not crazy at all.

Most people value marriage and permanancy in

marriage. When marriages end, particularly in divorce, people find themselves with a big "value gap" in their lives. They have, after all, given a lot of their life-energies to that value, and now it is gone. They often feel cheated, as if the value itself betrayed them.

They begin to double check their other values. Church attendance. Prayer. Continence outside of marriage. Parenting. Dress and appearance. People want to test all their other values lest they also betray. One way to test these values is to let them go for a while.

Although most people test values in this way, most are not clearly conscious of the process. They simply know that, some months after their marriages have ended, they are different. They are different because they have relinquished or modified some values. They may also have reclaimed some values and newly discovered others.

This shifting and sorting of values can be one of the most frightening parts of grief. Values form a kind of solid ground on which people build and shape their lives. During this period after the end of marriage, however, the ground turns to water. And not many of us can walk on water! Their very confusion then becomes a cry: "Lord, save me. I drown!"

What these struggling people need from others during this time is understanding. What they don't need is condemnation. They are, after all, struggling for integrity. God cannot but be pleased with that willingness to struggle.

Pal's Story

In one part of my story—the part where I was married for 33 years to the person I loved most of all—my sexual fulfillment was complete both emotionally and physically. I took this fulfillment for granted and never reflected on it. Since I've become a widow, however, I have reflected on my life—on whether I am a "whole" person as I try to make the change from a "we" existence to an "I" existence.

Although I felt loved and wanted in my childhood, I did not feel free to display emotions. We were not a touching family, and I often longed for that kind of relationship. It was Woody who taught me that it was all right to have a touching relationship with family and friends. In my marriage to Woody, I felt loved, touched, cared for, needed, wanted and trusted. And I responded in the same manner. In time, showing affection in marriage became as natural to me as *not* showing it had been in my childhood.

After Woody's death, I wondered how our friends, who were all couples, would accept me without Woody. I thought they would feel awkward. Or else I would feel awkward. I even misjudged their acceptance of me as a whole person. When they called me or touched me, I would think it was pity instead of sincerity and love.

The realization that, after all these years, I was vulnerable to distrust caused confusion in me and a lack of confidence. When I was with a group of friends, I would often be almost overwhelmed with insecurity. I wanted to touch and to be touched, but I felt restricted and wondered if I could risk their misunderstanding. I withdrew from our friends.

I began to feel like I was in a vacuum. I lived day to day doing just what I had to do with no desire to venture into anything more.

Then I became aware that my sexual feelings were reawakening. During the time Woody had been sick and for a while after his death, I didn't have any of these feelings. I felt confused and frightened by them now. As I looked at other widows, I felt almost ashamed and even more alone. They seemed to have it all together, to have everything under control. And they certainly never discussed anything so personal as their sexual feelings.

I didn't know how to cope with these feelings within me. I knew what my moral values were, so I knew what I wouldn't do. But I didn't know what I *would* do!

In my attempt to cope, I tried many different solutions. At first, I went to work in my oldest son's new dental office. I worked long hours. He would beg me to quit and get some rest, but I knew how lonely I'd be at home. No one knew how I hated to go into that bedroom alone. So I worked hard, hoping that I'd be so tired I could fall into bed and into at least a fitful sleep.

But that didn't work. As soon as my head would hit the pillow, I'd be wide awake. I'd sit straight up in bed, unable to relax and lie down. It was electrifying and frightening.

Then I'd try reading. I had always read a lot at night, and I thought that old habit would come to my aid. I would get up, collect some books and magazines, and go into the den and try to read myself to sleep.

Many times I considered mixing myself a drink during these long nights. But each time, I stopped myself. I was afraid that such an easy way out would have long-lasting unpleasant results. I vowed that I would never drink while I was alone.

I said many an agonizing prayer asking God to help me through one more night. Would the rest of my life be like this—so frustrating, lonely, futile? I felt trapped in a situation I had never dreamed of being in.

Somehow the days and nights passed. Very gradually, sleep returned. I began to relax.

One day, while in church, a particular hymn brought a rush of unexpected tears. As we were leaving, a friend came up to me and just held my hand. He didn't say a word. He didn't have to. That kind of feeling and caring has been one of the greatest helps to me.

I began to realize that the dear friends who had been "ours" were still "mine." They opened their hearts and arms to me and, by doing so, they helped me restore faith in myself as well as in them.

I also met a group of women and men who had all lost a spouse. Being able to tell them exactly how I felt helped boost my self-confidence. I no longer felt so isolated. For a while, I had thought I was the only widowed person to have strong sexual feelings. By sharing with these friends, I learned that many others have the same kind of feelings.

Sometimes the old pain pays me a surprise visit. My daughter-in-law, Sheri, often calls to tell me when there is a good movie on television. If it is a tender love story, it will still make my heart ache—so much so that, at times, I want to throw my shoe at the TV set. It is at those times I know my sexual feelings are not dead and my loneliness is not over.

I can't say just when it happened. All I know is that it is getting better. Just knowing I am not alone and not "different" helps me. And I am thankful for all the wonderful people who have loved me, hugged me, listened and been patient with me.

Sue's Story

When the priest pronounced Gary and me husband and wife, I knew I had found the man with whom I would share the rest of my life. He and I would fulfill and affirm each other emotionally and physically. When we needed to be reassured of our sexuality, we would look to each other for that reassurance.

Our physical relationship was satisfactory for most of the years we were together, but the emotional bond between us weakened as time passed. We did not share our feelings and private thoughts, and I often felt that we were strangers.

As we grew farther apart emotionally, I placed more and more emphasis on the physical aspect of our relationship. I thought that could make up for the emotional distance between us. But when we made love, the gap between us seemed almost to disappear.

My values at that time were well defined. We were married and, no matter what happened, we would be faithful as man and wife.

Even when I learned of Gary's relationship with another woman, I couldn't believe it meant the end of our marriage. I kept clinging to that value of permanency in marriage. When Gary ultimately chose to end the marriage, it seemed like everything I had believed in toppled and crashed.

The only other time I had suffered the loss of someone I cared for was when my father died. He had been missing for a couple of days. Gary and my brothers had been out looking for him while my mother and I waited at home for some word. I was standing in the entryway of the house I had grown up in when Gary came through the door. He put his arms around me and gently said, "They found him. He's dead, Sue." He held me as I cried. I had depended on Gary's love and support to comfort me. Now I had lost Gary and I needed someone to hold and comfort me again. But this time, it was different. I felt completely alone in my grief.

Suddenly the things I had valued up to that point—marriage, fidelity, commitment—meant nothing to me anymore. I had tried them and they hadn't worked. I knew only one thing for sure: I didn't want to be alone. I needed someone to help me through this, but there was no one.

The weeks that followed were awful. Making it

through the day was hard, but as the sun would begin to set, a hush would seem to fall over everything and loneliness would steal over me until I felt frantic. I would try to lose myself in the television shows, but most of the time I was too restless for much of that. Sleep might have been an answer, but the thought of climbing into that empty bed only made me more aware of how alone I was.

After a few weeks of that unbearable loneliness, I felt a compulsion to do something I had never dared to do before. I decided I had to get out, loosen up. So one night, frightened but driven by an overpowering need to be close to someone, I went out alone to a bar near the place where I worked.

As I drove up to the bar and turned off the car's engine, I found myself justifying my being there. "I can have a drink if I want. There's nothing wrong with that. Men do it all the time, so why can't a woman?"

I was wearing my sunglasses and when I opened the door everything was dark. I missed the step inside and stumbled. That was my graceful beginning of a different life-style! After regaining my balance, I stood there a moment until my eyes adjusted to the dim light inside. Then I quickly found a seat at the bar and nervously rummaged through my purse for a cigarette.

The bartender brought my order and my hands shook as I sipped my drink. But after a couple of drinks, the shaking had stopped, and by that time a man had taken the seat next to me. He struck up a conversation, and my alcohol-induced confidence allowed me to respond. That night I didn't have to be alone.

For many months after that, I felt like a changed person. I had found a way to be close to someone without the risk of being hurt again. The thought of becoming emotionally involved with anyone frightened me, so I kept every encounter on a purely physical basis. I never went with the same man twice.

The thought of right or wrong didn't enter my mind. What I was doing was totally foreign to everything I had believed in all my life, but none of that seemed to apply to me anymore. It took me a while to realize that, while I was gratifying my physical needs, I was turning my back on all my emotional needs.

In time, the emptiness caught up with me.

I began to experience a great deal of guilt and confusion. I missed having a personal relationship. I was not progressing through my loss. In fact, I was regressing. What's more, my behavior was destroying any chance to get in touch with my emotional needs. I began to realize that, if I continued on this path, I would never be truly close to anyone.

To say that I immediately put a stop to seeking only physical gratification would be untrue. It just wasn't that easy for me to change my behavior. When I would try to quit, the loneliness would cause me to panic; and I would start back to the bar. I knew my behavior was destructive, but so was my loneliness. I wrestled with these feelings for months.

Finally, very gradually, I began to redefine what was right for me in my single-again state. One-night stands were not right for me. I have a strong need for physical intimacy, but meeting *only* that need does not fulfill me. I also require other kinds of intimacy, the kind that allows people to really know me and to touch me and that allows me to know and touch others. One-night stands were directly opposed to fulfilling these needs.

Gradually, I stopped that pattern of behavior and tried to find ways to have my other needs met.

Fortunately I met some women who, like me, are single again. These women have become close friends. They, too, have felt the loneliness and frustration I have experienced. I have been able to confide to these friends my behavior and my feelings. It has been a great relief to me to have them listen without judging me. They accept my behavior as part of my pain.

I found it easy to develop friendships with women who were single again. It was more difficult for me to open up to men on a deep feeling level. It was difficult, but not impossible. As I came to know some men whose marriages had ended by death or divorce, I learned that they, like me, struggled with the tension between values and physical frustrations. They, too, wanted someone to listen to them and to understand. I found that I could have a genuine friendship with some of these men.

One man became a very special friend. Tom was divorced and had custody of his two children. He was my age, a tall, quiet, unpretentious man with a shy smile and a subtle but sharp sense of humor.

The friendship that developed between us did not involve physical expression. It was an outgrowth of our mutual need to share experiences and feelings. We would sometimes pile our combined children in the car and go out for ice cream. We spent lots of time talking. Tom is remarried now. I am happy to know that our friendship helped him work through his loss and prepare for a new beginning.

Honest friendships like the one with Tom have helped fill the void in my life. It's a joy as well as a great relief to have good friends and deep sharing without being afraid I'll be misunderstood.

I still have periods of longing for the physical gratification I became accustomed to during my marriage. Sometimes I feel envious of couples who seem affectionate. But now that I am more comfortable with my life as a single person, I can put these old feelings into perspective.

As long as I am caught up living life as fully as I can, I am more at peace.

Gene's Story

During my formative years, there was very little conversation or factual information concerning sexual matters directed my way by anyone. Nothing direct came from my parents; sex education certainly wasn't taught in the school I went to; and believe it or not, sex was only lightly suggested in movies and magazines. I got the definite impression that the topic of sex had best be left alone. It was better to live in wonderment than to shock or to embarrass anyone by bringing up the subject. My understanding of my own sexuality was blurred and undefined.

As I matured, pieces of the puzzle began to fall haphazardly into place, but the whole picture did not emerge until I was married.

In our marriage, Blanche and I were free to express complete intimacy with each other. Both physical and emotional intimacy. Despite my lack of sex education, I found sexual intimacy in marriage to be natural and good.

Earlier, Sue, Pal, Earl and I wrote about trust in our lives. In thinking about the trust in my life, I can honestly say that not once did I experience broken trust in my marriage. Not once! In our 25 years of marriage, in fact, trust was so basic that it never even occured to me that it *could* be broken. Somehow our backgrounds, our upbringing and the love we found in each other turned out to be the right combination of our mutual, almost naive trust. I'm sure this trust had a lot to do with the joy we experienced in physical intimacy.

In the twinkling of an eye on that snowy November day, the life of this beautiful person, my wife, was snuffed out like the flame of a candle. I felt that, right along with her death and the death of our marriage that resulted, a large part of me died, too. Not only did I lose a loved one, I also lost the concept of who I was. All of a sudden, I was only "half a couple"; and in my mind that made me a misfit in society. As half a couple, I had lost my sexual partner and the one to whom I could so completely express my total sexuality.

I was so emotionally drained in the days that followed Blanche's death that I was affected physically. A sort of vacuum existed inside of me. My sexual feelings seemed to vanish. I made no conscious effort to suppress them; they just went away. I remember not really caring then if they would ever come back again.

Christmas came just a few weeks later, and it just added to my emptiness and loneliness. I remember so well the feeling of longing for Blanche as I opened a Christmas gift she had bought and wrapped for me before she had left on her trip and which we had found hidden away in a closet. I missed her closeness, her touch, her soothing voice. I missed holding her hand at Midnight Mass, the "public" kisses under the mistletoe, and the very private, intimate times when Mr. and Mrs. Santa Claus found fulfillment in each other's embrace. If only I could have had one more hour with her, to touch her, to tell her the things that were in my heart, and to say the goodbye that I had not had the chance to say.

It was after the holiday season that I was forced back into the reality of living. Joan, our second eldest, was ending the Christmas break from her job which required continuous traveling. Ann, our middle daughter, was beginning a new semester at college. It was back to school also for Kathleen and Lori. And my own work could not be neglected any longer.

Around this time, I noted that my sexual feelings began to reappear. It began to sink in too that, like it or not, I was single again for the first time in 25 years. And the whole world was so much different from what it was the last time I was single. It seemed that the moral values I had followed all my life were taken so lightly anymore. Casual sexual behavior was explained away as "sexual freedom."

All of a sudden, I found myself at the same crossroad where my daughters were. It seemed crazy now, that after being so certain of my advice to them about morality, values and the proper development of their sexuality that I would now be in such a confused and uncertain state. It had certainly been easy to dish out words of wisdom from my secure little perch. But suddenly, I wasn't an observer anymore.

How I hated facing up to the facts that needed facing. How I dreaded getting into that lonely bed at night. How often I would let my mind wander to various women as potential sexual partners. And how strong was my desire to be physically satisfied again. I wondered if out there somewhere there was someone with whom I could develop the same kind of relationship that Blanche and I had had. I wondered if I would be willing to risk that much again.

I even had something return to me that I had almost forgotten about: nocturnal emissions. Wet dreams, they are commonly called. How frustrated that made me feel. How angry. To think that I could control so little now when just a short time back such problems were the farthest thing from my mind.

I had no answers. I couldn't see any worthwhile

future. All I could think of was the good past.

I found myself fighting going to bed until I was exhausted. And then I would keep my radio going softly all night for "company." It wasn't much help, but it was all I had.

Slowly I came to realize that the situation wasn't going to change. If any changing was to be done, it would have to be in me. I began to look realistically at myself and to reconsider my values. I saw society's view of sexual freedom, and I wondered about that and my own single-again state. What were my values now that my marriage vows no longer applied?

The more I thought about all this, the more I realized that the values I had talked about and lived were really deep in me. To me, only a strong bond of commitment and a deep and lasting relationship between a man and a woman is a solid enough foundation for sexual intercourse. I realized that the type of commitment I want comes only in a marriage relationship where there *can* be complete trust of one another and where the freedom to express feelings can be so much more than just physical.

The conclusions I have reached do not allow me to satisfy all my needs for physical intimacy, and I miss that part of life very much. The physical enjoyment in my marriage was important to me, but so were all the other satisfactions. I realize now that there are other ways that I can partially fulfill my need for intimacy.

I am aware that there are lots of ways in which people can express emotional and physical closeness. In my youth, my family was not a very touching family, but I really didn't think too much about it then. After I married, Blanche and my children took care of 99 percent of my emotional and physical needs. Now Blanche is gone. I continue to express my care for my daughters, and I feel emotionally close to them. These are parental expressions, and I am comfortable with them. Something not so comfortable for me was my reaction to being touched by women who were in the same state I was in—single again.

One of the satisfactions in my marriage had been the knowledge that my relationship with Blanche was secure and would continue until death at an old age. No more dating games to play. No more wondering if I could live with this one or that one. With Blanche I had had all my answers. It had felt secure and comfortable.

Now all of a sudden I was shoved out of this comfortable position. I didn't even want to think about beginning another search. I didn't like anything that looked like it meant starting that search again. I wondered what my reaction would be to a woman deliberately touching my arm. The feeling of her hand on my shoulder or in my hand. Her arm around my waist in a hug. And this woman not my wife? I was cautious. I drew some bounds within which I felt safe.

In the past few months, I have relaxed a little. I have learned that I can have a good friendship without its having to be a romance. Within my "comfortable zone," I now find that a hug, a kiss, a pat on the back and other such simple contacts are satisfying for me to give and even more satisfying to receive. I find that I can affirm another person as being okay in a number of ways, and that I can also be affirmed. Now that I am more aware of where I have drawn the line in these simple friendships, I feel sure that, if I should find someone crowding me, I could more easuly handle the situation.

To me, sex and sexuality are two different things. Yet there is a great intertwining of emotional needs with physical needs. Both needs are special gifts that God has given me to move me closer to other people. I am thankful that I have regained some trust in meeting these needs and yet remaining true to my values. I no longer consider myself "half a couple." And I no longer try to be "mother and father" to my daughters. My sexuality does not allow it. My children know they have a father, but they are motherless.

I have never been hesitant about doing household chores. You know, things like mopping floors, dusting, cooking, grocery shopping, scouring out commodes, and all the other things sometimes referred to as "woman's work." To me, that has nothing to do with sexuality. Right now it has a whole lot to do with just plain old survival. I accept it as one of the requirements of living, just as Blanche accepted it.

I still miss physical satisfaction, but I now know that not having sex does not mean I have to stop being a sexual person. One thing that has helped me to get a lot of this in perspective is a talk on sexuality I had occasion to give not long ago. The thinking, the writing, and the saying of the words helped me put it in a form I could hold onto. Doing this has given me a certain feeling of release: freedom to do things, to say things, to express my feelings in various ways, to let others know I care, to embrace, to kiss. I think this is the real Gene emerging—truly me, the way I believe God wants me to be—a man who is warm and caring.

Earl's Story

In thinking back on my marriage, I've come to realize how frustrated I was sexually. For a long time, I wouldn't admit this. I would hate to try counting the times since my divorce that I have set up a mental picture of Nancy and me together. These pictures would be followed by much anger knowing that I had been replaced by someone else. Thinking about this was one way I hung onto my past.

I know now how mismatched Nancy and I were. I'm an affectionate person. I like holding hands, kissing and little things like sitting beside someone with our legs touching. In my marriage, I was broken of all these dirty habits. There was no kissing, no hugging, no affectionate little pats and definitely no mention of love.

Love-making had to be carefully planned during my marriage. Permission was usually granted the day before in a bargaining session. I would almost always have to promise to do something out of the ordinary. One incident that comes to my mind involved a new car.

Now I have to admit that car salesmen are not one of my favorite kinds of people, and the man we were dealing with in the small office was slick and had shiftiness written all over him. The first thing he did was to prove how stupid I was. He told me that the car I was about to buy would definitely be worth more in three years than what I was about to pay for it. He also said that the car I purchased three years earlier wasn't worth anything. That had been a bad year for cars. I listened to all this for a while, and then I stood up and commenced giving him a good cussing. We left in the old piece of junk that just the day before we called a car!

In the car, Nancy told me how embarrassed I had made her feel, and then very quietly told me not to expect any sex with her for a long time.

I turned the car around, found my friendly car dealer, and agreed to buy the new car and give him my old one. Then I apologized to Nancy. I guess there wasn't much I wouldn't do for the sexual pleasures of my wife!

After my divorce, I didn't even have a chance to bargain.

For a long time after my divorce, I didn't feel good about sex. In fact, I didn't feel right about dating. For some reason, it made me feel as if I were cheating. My divorce proceedings took six months, and during that time Nancy got a boy friend. I can admit now that it was all right, but at the time, just the thought of her with someone else upset me to no end. I can remember how furious I got just thinking about it. I decided that if she could go and do goodness knows what, I could do the same. So I would make a date. But I couldn't go. Sometimes I would stand my date up without so much as a phone call. Even after the divorce was final, I would do this. I think the reason was that, deep down, I felt we were still married.

I have to admit that I was pretty loyal to and beyond the end of my marriage.

One of the things that upset me the most was when Nancy would be sincere and say, "Earl, what you need to do is to go out and find you a nice girl-friend." Hearing that from her would almost kill me.

During that time, I wasn't married and I couldn't make myself date. I would go places and look at couples and when I would see a pleasant looking couple, I would say to myself, "I bet I could love her more than he does." I felt all good women were either married or already spoken for. I would feel very lonely. Finally I decided to take Nancy's advice to go out and find a girlfriend.

But I didn't know where to look or how to go about it. The first place I looked was at bars, and I had no trouble finding some "friendly" women.

Later I began to go with a different kind of woman. She was a good woman and I liked her company. The men I knew at the bar were no different from the boys I had grown up with. If I had a date, they would ask me the next day, "How did you do?" And sometimes I would find myself lying just as kids do.

I didn't want to tell these men the truth about how awkward I had felt the night before, standing at the woman's door, just shaking her hand and giving her a slight good-night peck. And I couldn't tell these men how good it made me feel to think that the next day at work the woman was telling her friends about the unusual man she had dated—a man who wouldn't even hold her hand!

This relationship was good, but it didn't satisfy me. I knew that one of the reasons that I hurt so much was that I had so much love to give and it seemed as if nobody wanted it. Nancy had even told me that one of the reasons for our divorce was that it wasn't fair for me to go through life with a woman who didn't love me. She said I was too good a man for that. I remember my reply to her. "It doesn't make any difference if you love me or not because I've got enough for both of us." She didn't want it. Now I was bound and determined to find someone who wanted all the love I had to give. I began to want to fall in love with someone.

I did find a person to whom I was very attracted, and I fell madly in love with her. She gave me something I had never had before. We touched, kissed and held each other almost constantly. Everything about this relationship was different from the way my marriage had been. I found out that sex did not have to happen when the dishes were all done, the kids were all asleep and the 10:15 weather had gone off TV. I was so thrilled with this new experience that I called my ex-wife and sincerely thanked her for divorcing me! As soon as I hung up the phone, though, I realized that my relationship with my new friend was over. It has lasted a little more than a week!

I had lots of mixed feelings about this. It felt good

to know that someone could really love and care for me. And then I felt bad because I couldn't care for her. I was heartbroken because I felt I could never love anyone again. I began to think something was wrong with me. I was also ashamed. I didn't know how to end the relationship. I felt like I had lied to my friend by telling her that I loved her. I had said that to only one other woman in my life, and that woman had been Nancy. I made the mistake of letting the affair drag on two more months because I wasn't man enough to end it properly. The way I handled it was by drinking and feeling like a rat. I tried to make her hate me. I finally told her one night that I didn't think I loved her and that she was too good to go through life with someone who didn't love her.

For a long time after this, I refused to do any more dating.

I have begun to realize a lot of things about myself in my relationship to women. Sometimes I say to myself and to others that I don't like women. But I'm beginning to think that deep down I'm afraid of them. I don't ever want to be hurt or rejected like I have been; and in order to avoid the danger of this happening again, I've become very stand-offish. When I'm around a person who seems to me unavailable, I'm a completely different person. I can talk. I can laugh, and even sometimes be fun.

I think it only fair to admit that I do have values and I also have an active sex life. I hear people say that they cannot understand one-night affairs, and sometimes I shake my head in agreement. But I know good and well that one-nighters are all I can handle right now. I am a man with physical needs, and as long as I don't hurt anyone, I don't think there's anything wrong with satisfying those needs. And if there's anything I feel guilty about, it's not feeling guilty! When I hear somebody like Gene, I sometimes think I *ought* to feel guilty.

I've also come to realize that I need friendship. I have come to know and trust a few women in friendship. I have discovered that I can have friendship with a woman without having sex.

Maybe someday I can find someone with whom I can fulfill both these needs, my need for sex and my need for friendship. Maybe someday I can marry again. But right now I doubt if I ever will.

Reflections

Pal and Gene, Earl and Sue had to find a new balance in life after their marriages ended. They had somehow to bring harmony into the conflict between their sexual needs and their moral values. Their ways of coping were influenced by the experiences of marital intimacy they had had.

Gene had enjoyed full sexual intimacy up until Blanche's death. The loss of his sexual partner was sudden and absolute. Blanche had been his best friend. In fact, she had been his only intimate friend. So he first experienced her absence as loss of friendship. For a time, his genital feelings were stunned into lifelessness. It was some weeks after her death that he began to feel his loss as a physical frustration. At Christmas, when he opened his gift from her, he longed first for her emotional presence. It was then that he consciously missed the long-practiced physical intimacy they had enjoyed. From then on, he experienced her absence as a *total* loss of intimacy—both physical and emotional.

Because of Woody's prolonged illness, Pal's loss was not as abrupt as Gene's was. Pal had already adjusted to a diminished expression of physical intimacy. She could touch Woody, rub his back and massage his temples. She did not miss having full physical unity, because she was secure in their emotional closeness. At least, she didn't miss that at first. Like Gene, her genital feelings seemed to have died when the marriage ended. Their reawakening bothered her and intensified the emotional loss she felt.

Things were different with Earl. His marriage had not been satisfactory on either an emotional or a physical level. Nancy had not loved him. They had gotten along, but they had not had a deep, sharing friendship. Their marriage was not life-giving on an emotional level. Earl didn't realize this lack until later. He was somewhat more aware of the dissatisfaction in their physical intimacy. But in Earl's mind, the marriage was permanent. He tried to make the best of the situation without reflecting on it too much.

Perhaps the lack of emotional closeness and his own strong need for intimacy caused Earl to emphasize in his mind the importance of physical love-making in his marriage. It was a way to experience at least in that one dimension the unity he longed for. Yet the incongruence made even that unsatisfactory.

In reality, then, Earl didn't lose profound intimacy, for he never had it profoundly. His loss was in degree. It went from vaguely unsatisfactory to destructive.

Early in her marriage, Sue had experienced congruent sexual intimacy with Gary, a closeness that was both physical and emotional. But very soon, the emotional unity began to fade. So even though their physical love-making continued, there was a gap in the intimacy.

In both Sue's and Earl's situations, physical unity was more-than-ordinarily important because it had to bear the whole weight of married intimacy. It was not only a physical closeness but also a substitute for emotional closeness or friendship.

How did these four persons reenact their sexual losses?

Earl had actually experienced personal rejection long before his divorce. When Nancy said she didn't love him, he offered love enough for both of them. He was turned down. He had had to "bargain" in order to be received just physically. He could make no bargain in order to be received emotionally.

Earl reenacts that rejection to this day. He says he cannot enter into a fully sexual relationship with one person. In this way, he continues to live out his rejection.

When he did become emotionally and physically

involved with one woman, he did to her what Nancy had done to him. In fact, he said almost the same words Nancy had said: "You're too good to go through life with someone who doesn't love you."

This is not to say that Earl *should* have continued his relationship with the woman he met after his divorce. Quite possibly it was too soon for him to enter into a permanent relationship at that time. But the way he handled it was almost like a textbook example of substitution. "A woman treated me this way, so I'll treat a woman the same way."

He is several steps beyond that now. For one thing, he has done a lot of honest reflection. He sees his former marriage in a more realistic way. For another thing, he sees and admits his own fear of being hurt by a woman. To admit such fears is the first step in defeating them. And finally, he has developed, for the first time in his life, some genuine friendships with women. All these steps put Earl in a good place. He no longer has to reenact his rejection. He now has more freedom to determine his future.

Sue's husband had pulled back from emotional unity even while he continued to have a physically gratifying relationship with her. After the divorce, Sue reenacted that relationship pattern by pulling back from any kind of emotional closeness. If her friendship had not been acceptable to Gary, then it surely wouldn't be acceptable to other men. She had been rejected, and she reenacted that rejection by doing what she had done in her marriage: substituting her body for her being. At least that brought some sort of acceptance.

During the months in which Sue followed this behavior, she temporarily let go of her moral values. For a time, her need for acceptance in physical intimacy won out over her need for intact values. But only for a time. She discovered that—for her—life without those values was too painful. Sue has now come to a point where she is able to integrate her values and her sexual needs. Her situation is not without loneliness and physical frustration. But she's back on firm ground.

As far as overt behavior is concerned, Pal's seemed never to waver. The values she held before Woody's death are the values she holds now. But, the fact is that Pal has done a lot of shifting in her value network. She values herself as an individual in a way she didn't do before widowhood. She has a new kind of trust in the affection of others. She has been tempted to withdraw, to drink her problems into oblivion, to overwork. She has resisted all three temptations. Even at the risk of scandalizing other widowed persons, she has taken a clear look at her sexuality and has declared her sexual frustrations and her need for intimacy. Pal has found *degrees* of intimacy that correspond to her moral values.

Gene's relationship with Blanche was so good that it would be easy for him to fall into the reenactment pattern of idealizing her in order to remain cut off from intimacy. Her death ended their unity in as absolute way; her idealization could keep it absolutely ended. But Blanche was a woman, not a plaster-of-paris saint. She left Gene the gift of knowing how good it is to be intimate. It would be a compliment to her if he seeks that kind of intimacy again.

Gene has taken a new look at himself and at the values he had taken so long for granted. Gene will live in continence outside of marriage. That value held up. But he has added some new ones. He is much more tolerant and understanding of others— even when their behavior and values run counter to his. He and Earl, for example, are very special friends. Gene could not live according to Earl's values and behavior, but he can accept Earl and he appreciates Earl's real and unique goodness. In the past, Gene valued having everything in perfect order around his home. He has modified that value in favor of spending more time helping other persons who have lost a spouse.

Gene will form many life-giving friendships. And in doing this, he will be living out his sexuality in a real, if somewhat limited way.

On one level, Earl and Gene, Sue and Pal have told the story of how they are coping sexually in their single-again situation. On another level, they have told about seeking integrity. Integrity is not so much a condition as it is a process. They are all still in that process. That's a holy and human place to be in the journey called life.

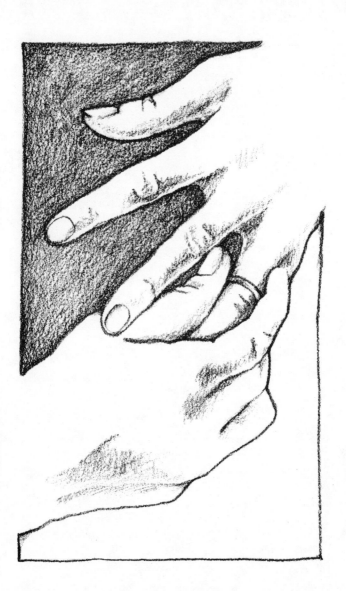

4. Closing Doors on the Past

When people are in the throes of grief, they are inclined to talk—if they talk at all—in circles. They *think* in circles. And it is the unpleasant habit of circles to move endlessly around and around in their own paths. Fundamentally, the circle during grief goes like this: "I am miserable today; I can't bear to think of tomorrow; it's all because of what happened in the past." Obviously, this circle of thought keeps bringing people back to their pasts.

They are chained to the past when they spend too much time reliving it in their memories, when they use the past to excuse unsuitable present behavior, when they ignore the present and refuse to face the future.

Probably the most telltale sign of bondage to the past is the habit of directing a disproportionate amount of emotional energy back there. Divorced persons may channel their anger against their former spouses with so much intensity that they have little or no emotion left for the present. Widowed persons may find an emotional outlet in the form of nostalgia or despair.

In any case, as long as people remain emotionally bound to a person or event of the past, they cannot get on very well with living in the here and now. They keep spinning around the same circle.

What is the way out? Closure. People whose marriages have ended need to close the door on the past. If they slam the door in anger, it will bounce back open. If they just nudge it indecisively, it won't close. They need to come to a point where they are able to close the door very firmly, very gently.

Closure requires a decision to do three things: first to accept the past for what it is; second, to shift into a kind of emotional neutral gear concerning the past; and third, to become actively involved in new life in the present.

First, accept the past. Acceptance neither denies the past nor blots it out of memory. It faces the past and says, "Yes, this is what happened. These parts are regrettable; these other parts are good. It has happened, and now it is part of my unique story." Acceptance also enables people to step free from the ceaseless habit of remembering.

Second, shift into neutral. People can *decide* to become more calm and objective about their former life-styles and spouses. This power of decision does not mean that they should—or even that they can—deny feelings of anger and sadness. Negative feelings are part of grief. They will come and they should be owned. They need to run their course. That's exactly the point: Once they have run their course, people can decide whether to re-run them or to let them go.

Third, become involved in new life. That simply means that people open their eyes to the people and situations around them. It means that they begin to take care of themselves. They begin to pay attention to others. Today offers its own things to see, voices to hear, people to touch, risks to take. Widowed and divorced people can, if they choose, respond to these present realities with feeling. Even when the feeling hurts. At least they know that emotion spent in the present is a sign of life!

Acceptance of the past, objectivity toward the former spouse, involvement in the present: these are the ways to move toward closure as well as the signs that one is, in fact, closing.

On paper, it sounds like a neatly ordered process. But of course it isn't. Closure is neither ordered nor easy. Like grief itself, closure is irregular and painful.

Some people never close the door on their pasts; others do. But there comes a point when bondage or freedom is a matter of choice. The choice may not be easy. And following through may be downright agonizing! But people can choose.

Choice is not always traceable to a pin-point moment in time. It can be made so quietly and so gradually that it is almost imperceptible. But whether people make their decision consciously or sub-consciously, they are responsible for their own freedom or bondage. If they choose freedom, its coming may be ever so subtle. Then one day they will be surprised to discover they have new life.

New-life events require rituals.

Deep within us, we have a human need to ritualize turning points in our lives. It is like an ancient instinct in humankind. Some rituals, like some choices, rise up from some place deeper in us than consciousness. The ritual usually involves some semi-public statement of the turning point.

There are rituals for marriage. There are rituals for death and burial. Those are more or less standardized rituals. Many widowed and divorced persons seek some kind of simple ritual when they close the door on the past. It might be taking off the wedding ring, changing a name, moving to a different house, changing their style of dress, writing a letter, composing a poem.

Where do people find the power to choose life again when grief strikes them down? From the Source of Life.

When God bent over that first damp clay figure and breathed himself into it, the figure stirred to life bearing the image of God. Just as God called the first woman and man to life, so he *continues* to call his daughters and sons to come alive. The power of God-in-us is the power that enables people to move through grief to creative acceptance.

In that power, they can close on the past and open to the present. They can end their grief with life-giving acceptance. To do this is holy because it is a choice to live. It is a choice to say yes to the breath of God.

Sue's Story

One cold day in February of this year, the children

and I were snowbound at home. We had all tired of watching television, and they had asked me if we could look at our home movies. I hadn't thought of those movies in years. They had all been taken when the boys were small. We agreed it would be fun to see them.

Popcorn had to be made first. Who ever heard of watching movies without it? Then the boys got the canisters of film while I tried to recall how to operate the projector.

Finally we were ready. The four kids and our three dogs were settled in front of me on the living room floor, munching popcorn and staring expectantly at the blank white wall we would use as a screen. Tony handled the lights. I threw the switch. And we all sat back to enjoy the production.

As I saw Mike and Tony cavorting on the wall at the ages of three and one, my first thoughts were of how they had grown and what darling babies they had been. Then I remembered that I had taken those movies while Gary was in Vietnam so that he wouldn't miss this precious time of their lives. I felt a little sad because he misses so much of their lives now.

Then onto the wall came Gary, winking at me as I held the camera and giving me a sign that was a private joke between us. I laughed when I saw that sign, and the laughter felt good.

That night I realized that somewhere in the last two and a half years, I had lost much of the anger I had felt following our divorce. Watching those movies reminded me of the good times Gary and I had shared together in the past. That realization didn't change the fact that our life together was over. But I didn't cry myself to sleep remembering how things had once been. I had accepted the fact that we would never be together again. I had closed the door. Now I was moving on with my life.

Before I came to this point, my life had been tied to both the past and the future in a way that had rendered me practically immobile in the present. I would wake up in the mornings dreading the day that lay ahead because I was unsure of my abilities on the job and afraid of failure and criticism. During the day at work, I constantly checked and rechecked what I had done to be sure it was correct. Finally, I'd get through the day and start home. Driving home, a lump would rise in my throat at the thought of entering that house. I hated going home to the clutter. But I knew the children would be waiting for me, so I went.

I had no privacy in that two-bedroom house. The children slept in the bedrooms, and I slept on a couch in the dining room. There was no place I could go to be alone, so I would wait until everyone else was settled for the night. Then I'd wrestle with fear. Fear of losing my job, of alienating my children because of my lack of patience, of not having enough money to feed them properly, and on and on.

There in the darkness I would think of the years and years ahead of me as a single parent. The future would seem so bleak that I would fall into depression and anxiety. Sometimes I would remember how life had been before our divorce and I'd feel worse than ever.

The next morning I would wake up dreading the day, and the whole pattern would start over. I was tied to the past by memory and to the future by fear.

During that period of my life, it was impossible for me to make decisions. To make even a small decision meant dealing with the present, and that was too scary. It was even hard for me to pick up the phone and make an appointment for the children to go to the dentist. I worried that I wouldn't choose the right dentist or that I wouldn't be able to pay for the visit.

When I wasn't worrying about the future, I was filled with anger about the past. Gary had put me in this position. Oh, how I hated him then. He was responsible for all my misery, and he didn't seem to be suffering at all. If anger could have freed me from Gary, I would have been free then. But anger only kept me tied to him. All of my other emotions were blocked. I had room only for anger, and it was all directed backwards.

I can't say that I have lost all the negative feelings about the past and my worries about the future. When I sit alone some nights, even now, I think of how it will be when the kids are grown and gone. I will be alone then. Gary will have his wife to share those years with him. When I think of that, I feel cheated and very sad.

These feelings return at other times, too. When I have to take my car into the shop and have it repaired because I can't afford a new one, I feel angry because he has two new cars and I'm going broke on my old one. At times like these, I realize that I haven't made a complete closure on the past yet. But I've made a lot of progress.

I can't name a specific time when I decided to try to leave the past behind me and begin living in the present. It has been a gradual development.

I began by making decisions that affect my life in the present. One of the biggest decisions came when I found a house with three bedrooms, lots of space and a big backyard. I signed a lease for it. Then I decided to apply for a home loan to buy the house so we could put down roots and gain a sense of permanence and home. My first application for the loan was turned down, but I reapplied with a co-signer. Two years ago, I would not have thought I could ever make a big decision like that.

A few months after we moved, a friend presented me with an opportunity to change jobs. The pay was much better, but the responsibility was greater. The job called for more skills than I had acquired, and I was torn between my old fear of failure and a desire to better our financial situation. No one could make the decision but me. I decided to accept the position and trust my ability to learn what was required. So far, I've been able to function very well in the position. I'm proud of being able to do the job, but the thing I'm most proud of is deciding to *take* the job.

Decisions like these bring me smack up against the present. They help me leave the past in the past.

My children have provided the greatest impetus for my decision to begin living in the present with more courage. As long as I was wrapped up in worries about the future and anger about the past, I was passing up the present opportunity to share the "now" with my children. I was missing my chance to show them the love and care I have for them.

During this past summer, the children spent two months with Gary. While they were gone, I realized that where we live is only a house when they are not there. What makes it a home is family—the children and me being together, growing, sharing good times and bad.

The more I live with this kind of awareness in the present, the more I am closing on the past. And I savor my freedom at those times like when we sat down to watch our home movies.

Gene's Story

When the numbness began to wear off after Blanche's funeral, I found my whole being in an erratic state. My feelings would come and go without pattern. My thoughts of Blanche, our life together, my loneliness and bitterness occupied most of my waking hours. Our home, her picture, my wedding ring and a million other things constantly reminded me of the past and of my present unhappiness. The miserably cold winter we had that year didn't help any, either.

Sometimes a flash would come to my mind and I'd say to myself, "You'd better get hold of yourself, boy"; and I'd talk myself into feeling better. Unfortunately, the least thing would put me back in the doldrums and I'd be even more miserable. I'd think, "This is the way it will probably be from now on."

My mind would wander in a circuit—from the good past to my present unhappiness and back.

I would even let my imagination torture me. I would put myself at the accident scene, see Blanche's injuries, and desperately, futilely, try to prevent her death. I sometimes let my imagination take me through my own death. I would visualize myself standing before the almighty king and judge, and I could picture Blanche there. I had no wish for my own death then, but I really would not have cared if it happened. It was easy for me to see why some people would desire death at such a time.

I don't know if it was the emergence of spring after that severe winter or what, but I began to realize that I needed to find a release for myself. I wanted to take some larger steps on that journey back to my wholeness. I wanted to come back to life, to accept reality the way it was. I had no idea, though, how I could accomplish this. I found a way almost by accident.

Before Blanche had died, I had always looked forward to going home from work in the late afternoon. A good meal was usually in the making and it was great to be back on a personal and relaxed level with those I loved. But now with Blanche gone, coming home was nothing like it used to be.

One afternoon I arrived home and found the house empty. My daughters weren't home. No supper was cooking. I felt so lonely that tears welled up. With pen in hand, I stood at the chest of drawers in my bedroom and wrote a few brief lines on a piece of scrap paper. Things like: "Where are you?" "What's it like there?" "Do you know that I miss you?"

That's all it took to get my imagination racing again. I wondered why I had written those words down instead of just thinking them. Without being conscious of it, I had hit upon something that would help me make a closure on the past.

During this period of grief, I found myself sort of talking to Blanche, mostly in thought, but sometimes verbally, too. This came easily when I was in bed at night waiting for the sleep that always seemed to come so slowly. My thoughts often settled on the things I would like to tell her if only I could have just one more hour with her. How much I wanted to say the goodbye to her that I did not have the chance to say, to summarize all the feelings that had become a part of me because of my having known and loved her.

We have a redbud tree in our back yard. We planted it when it was just a sprig and, with special care and attention over the years, it increased in size and beauty. Blanche used to call it her "lavender popcorn ball" when it was in bloom, and I'll bet we have at least a hundred pictures of that tree.

Late that winter, while all the other trees still stood like skeletons, that tree came to life again and poured forth its beauty once more. Around that same time, I became aware of some restlessness within me, and I felt the urge to write something. I knew it had to be more than the brief thoughts I had written before. It had to be something that would satisfy this undefined need I had to move out of the past. It amazes me now that I ever thought of it, but I decided to write a letter to Blanche!

I took every precaution so that no one would know what I was doing—and that wasn't easy around my house! I had a hard time actually starting it, but that blooming redbud tree came to the rescue. I remember starting off my letter by commenting on how pretty her lavender popcorn ball was. I told her how surprised I was that it still had life in it. The way I'd been feeling, I wouldn't have been surprised if it had died during that miserable winter, too. I reminded her that the very last picture of our family together was taken under its lavender glow.

With that, the dam burst and I almost couldn't stop writing. That letter covered a span from the time I was a boy until the last day of my life—and even beyond. I wrote as best I could of my feelings of love for her, how much she had meant to me, and the privilege that was mine to have shared more than half my life with her. I apologized for my injustices toward her, and I forgave her for hers toward me. At last I bid her farewell, and I admitted to myself that, except for the memories, our past together was over.

Several unexpected things happened with regards to that letter. One was that I could not write her name on it. I hadn't put her name on at first for fear that someone might see it and realize what I was doing. After I finished the letter, I was unable to force myself to write her name on it.

Another problem was that I would read it over and over again, usually when I got home from work. Each time I read it, I felt sadness and I would drift backwards into our past. That letter was not the closure I had thought it might be. Instead it became for me a direct pathway back to yesterday. I wasn't yet ready to let go.

Activities around Easter interrupted this hangup of mine, and then another idea came to me. I had the desire to let someone else know about some of the things I had written to her. There was only one person to whom I could write this kind of letter, and that was Blanche's sister, Virginia, who lives in the Chicago suburbs. Like Blanche, Virginia had been a passenger in the ill-fated car. By this time, she had pretty well recuperated from her injuries. I felt I knew her well enough that she wouldn't misinterpret such a letter.

Using the letter to Blanche as a guide, I wrote what I am certain will always be the longest letter of my life. I had a lot to say, but I tried my best to keep it from becoming sad or depressing.

When I was finished, I destroyed my letter to Blanche and then debated with myself about mailing the more recent letter. When I found myself reading that one over and over just as I had done the first one, I decided I needed to mail it. For me, it was the right thing to do. That letter was so bulky that I had to mail it in a manila envelope and I remember that it took five 13-cent stamps to do it!

When I handed the envelope to the clerk at the post office, I remember a feeling of being through!

Of being done! My burden suddenly seemed lighter. A lot of the old me was in that envelope, and I was sending it far away.

Just as I had hoped she would, Virginia accepted my letter completely. She called me the weekend after she received it and we talked for a long time. She was understanding of my need to write it and appreciated my choosing her to receive it.

During the time I was writing those letters, I honestly did not know why I was doing it. I made sure no one knew what I was doing; I felt my sanity would be questioned. Since then, though, I realize that I was ritualizing a subconscious desire to make a closure on part of my past. I wasn't denying the past; I just wanted to stop living there.

I also realize now that my life is full of closures and fresh beginnings. When I left home, when I got married, when my parents died—all of those events demanded closures and new starts. My family of five daughters at home has now been reduced to two, and there have been lots of closures in the process. Colette and Joan because of marriage and Ann because of employment are now living in other towns. Their leaving home closed the door on the way life had been for us up to that point. My life moves on with its large and small closures.

My growing awareness and relationship with others who have suffered major losses has made me want to make some other kinds of closures, too: closures on some of the ways I used to be; on my former quickness to judge others unfairly; on my indifference and lack of caring when others were hurting; and on the narrow and self-serving style in which I formerly existed.

Good or bad, my past is gone forever and cannot be relived. I am thankful for the good memories it created, for the fruits it produced, and for the multitude of people who filled it. I acknowledge those things and savor them, but it is history. It is to the future that I look, a future where I can benefit from lessons learned from past mistakes, correct injustices and rearrange my priorities. It is to this kind of future that I wish to lay my claim.

Earl's Story

When I was married, one of the things I got very attached to was our dog. Her name was Sheba. I called her my Sheba-dog.

Sheba was of no one particular breed. She was just a big dog, a good, happy dog. We lived in a new development with very few houses. Sheba and another dog had the run of the whole countryside. She and her friend would chase rabbits and cows all day and coons at night. I could tell by her smell some mornings that they also chased skunks.

As more families moved into the area, our once-farmy neighborhood became sophisticated. Some of the new people were cultured and their dogs were pedigreed. To them it was unheard of to let a big mutt run free. So we had a six-foot cedar fence built around the backyard.

But after spending all her adult life running free, Sheba's animal instinct would not allow her to remain fenced in. She soon learned to climb the fence. Once out, she would become a terror to the dogs that had once been her friends.

We then had to chain her to a tree. But she soon learned that if she ran hard, she could hit the end of the chain with enough force to break it. I often saw her do that. She would hit the end of the chain so hard that it would twist her neck and flip her backwards. Surely she suffered for days each time she broke that chain, but to her it was worth those few hours of freedom.

Just as Sheba wanted the fields to roam in, I wanted my home to live in. I wanted to be with those inside. I wanted them to be mine again. Just as Sheba couldn't forget how things had been before she was chained up, neither could I.

I was fortunate to have been given a good memory, and with that memory I lived. Even though *I* felt sad when I thought of my family, I always pictured *them* in my mind as smiling. I could not block out all the good times.

After I would think of my family for a while, I would break out of my apartment and actually go back to what was once my home. I would ache for days every time I did this.

Going back would bring out all my sentimental feelings. I would drive up to the house and see the car that had taken my family to Alaska and back safely. I would think of how terrible the miles had seemed then, but how precious the memory of them was now. The black front door with the proud eagle on it had always been a welcoming sight, but now it was closed to me. For a while, the only entrance for me was by kicking it open. I'm ashamed to admit that I did that more than once.

The living room with its blue carpet and blue furniture always looked as if someone of importance was expected. The picture over the couch in the den had been an unexpected birthday gift from me to Nancy. I was still making payments on the television set. There was a massive pine table in the kitchen which we had acquired from my cousin and his wife after their divorce. Close to the table, a patio door opened onto the backyard where my Sheba-dog lived.

Nancy had decorated this home, and everywhere I looked I saw her. I thought of every little decision we had made about the house, and about how big each decision seemed at the time.

The bedroom was decorated in greens and held the king-sized bed in which two of our children were conceived. To this day, the thought of that bed makes me sad.

I would look over everything in the house and I could see special meaning in everything. I would say to myself, "It's not right that everything I've worked so hard for all my life is taken from me. And me left without so much as a picture of my kids." I felt as if an unexpected fire had raced through my life and taken my family and every other thing that had ever meant anything to me.

After Sheba broke her chain and ran free a few hours, we'd catch her and chain her back up. It was the same way with me. After a trip back to my house, I'd have to go back to my apartment and look at what I now called a home and would get sick. I knew I would hear no laughter. There would be no sounds of crying and no having to separate two kids fighting. This was when my phone would go in the ice box, and I would close off the outside world for days and live inside with my memories.

One incident that kept coming back in my memory was a time I was working in Altus, Oklahoma. We were trying to get two pieces of heavy metal bolted together. The machine holding the metal up was not strong enough, and just about the time we would get them lined up, the hydraulic cylinders would leak off and we would be back where we started from.

I don't have the greatest amount of patience, and I told Gary, a young man working for me, to stick his finger in the hole and tell me when it was lined up. He replied, "No. It might slip and cut my finger off."

Angrily I put my own finger in the hole just as the machine leaked off. I heard the crack and felt the numbness. But here again I refused to believe what had happened. I quickly closed my hand and refused to look at it. Even though I felt the blood oozing, I refused to admit it had happened. Gary was staring at me and finally asked, "Did it get you?" With no answer, I moved to the other side of the hole, got down on my knees, and from there I saw the other end of my finger. Then I replied, "I guess so."

All the way to the hospital, I refused to look. I didn't want to go to the hospital or to see a doctor. All I wanted to do was go home. If I could just go home, my finger would be all right. I could rub my hand on my kids and it would heal faster.

The sick feeling I had on the way to the hospital was the same feeling I had after my divorce. All I wanted was to go home. I could stand to look at the person I once was, but I refused to see the person I was now without my family. This time, though, there was no doctor, no hospital that could heal me. I could not take my hurt feelings to my children and make them go away.

A few months after my divorce, my Sheba-dog found a home on a farm in east Texas. It was a large farm where she had room to roam and play all she wanted.

After being cooped up in my apartment with my memories, I would begin thinking that I could find my farm somewhere other than here. I thought about moving away. I thought about running away. But I was wrong. I'm a person, not an animal. I have a choice where my home will be. Here is where I began and here is where I'll stay. The memories that kept me chained to the past would go with me wherever I went. Moving wouldn't free me.

I knew I would have to stop living in the past and begin to face the future, no matter how bleak it looked. The debts I had accumulated over the past one and a half years would have to be paid. The work I had quit would have to be taken up again. No matter how much I hated my apartment, I would have to accept it as my home. As long as I refused to face the future, my memories would keep me in the past. And I couldn't live there any more.

I went back to work. Almost everything I make goes to pay on my debts. But I accept this now.

Once in a while I'll keep a couple of hundred dollars in my pocket for a day or two just for the feel of it. But then I'll give it to my cousin who loaned me money. Making payments will be part of my future for some months to come. Maybe years. This I now accept.

I have begun to accept my apartment as my home. My home is not something found in a magazine, but all around I can see a splash of me. The other day, I noticed a little mound of dirt on the carpet beside one of my plants. Upon further investigation, I discovered that some ants were using the soil in my planter to build an ant hill right in my living room!

My little girl, Susan, had her 13th birthday a short time back. One of the things she wanted was for us to go as a family to a restaurant of her choice. We all agreed. This was maybe the best supper I had had with my family.

As I sat on one side of the table and Nancy on the other, it dawned on me that I would never be married to her again. This didn't mean that I didn't care for her. But I didn't feel a great amount of anger or of sadness. On the way home that evening, I felt single and I didn't despair. I realized then that I had really begun to let go of the past and to live in the present.

There are still some things that I find hard to accept. The coming home at night to an empty house. The loneliness at night and wanting to reach over and touch someone. Missing the sound of my kids. But I also know now that, with time, I will someday fully accept this.

Pal's Story

Several months after Woody's death, I was
awakened by his voice calling my name. I answered
and reached over to his side of the bed only to be
shocked into reality. I sat up in bed badly shaken,
sad, and very wide awake.

Were my dreams playing tricks on me? Or was I
losing my mind? This experience occurred more
than once, and I wondered how long this kind of
thing would torture me.

It was a long, slow journey through the grief to
peaceful acceptance. One thing that held me back
was guilt. I felt guilty for not having talked more
with Woody about death and parting. We had both
felt so alone during his sickness, and if I could have
talked with him, neither of us would have had to be
alone. After many months, I was able to rest in the
knowledge that God forgives my shortcomings if
only I will accept his forgiveness. Letting go of that
burden of guilt was a big step toward acceptance.

Farther along in my journey I was plagued with
depression. I was almost overwhelmed by my
feelings of inadequacy in trying to settle business
and estate affairs. Sometimes I would even say,
"Oh, why couldn't I have died with him?" But the
children would dispel that thought. They loved me
and needed me.

Another thing that held me in depression was the
sight of a married couple our age. Or I'd see some of
the men together who had served on the same
board with Woody. Why were they still here and
Woody gone? I wondered if I'd ever feel whole and

really happy again.

Working through grief toward acceptance dragged on and on. I was reluctant to close the door on our past, for that seemed like betraying Woody and denying our life together.

During the first year after Woody's death, I found many doors to close. Each birthday, our wedding anniversary, a certain song or prayer, our first grandchild, a joke, a trip to our cabin at the lake: whatever it was, it was the first time I'd experienced those things without Woody. Each event was a door to be closed. At each of those times, the ache would return and loneliness would engulf me. One painful incident would no sooner pass but another would arise. That year was like a thousand years. Many times I'd catch myself saying, "I must tell Woody that . . .," only to be stabbed again with the realization of the great void in my life.

The holidays of that first year were the most difficult time. Our youngest son, 14-1/2, was still at home, so I wanted to maintain the same traditions that he was accustomed to in our family.

On Thanksgiving, our whole family assembled the way we had always done. Everyone tried desperately to create a festive air. Some friends dropped by just as we were sitting down to eat. Upon my insistence, they joined us. Their presence helped us through the meal. I was unaware at the time that their visit at that hour was intentional. They knew I would be missing Woody at that family gathering.

Christmas was the next big hurdle. Each occasion seemed more like opening a door than closing one.

My daughter, Kathy, went shopping with me and that was a big help. But I wasn't really interested in buying gifts, and to this day I don't remember what I bought.

Then we had to buy a Christmas tree. Traditionally our whole family would go together to select the tree. It was an afternoon adventure, and I'm sure we drove the salesman crazy as the seven of us would race up and down the rows shouting at one another about the shapes and heights of different trees. It had always been such fun.

But this year, it was only Blake and me. The weather was turning very cold. Time was running out. Both of us were reluctant to go but we finally donned our heavy winter coats, climbed into the truck and braved the winter weather. Our hearts were so heavy that we couldn't carry on a conversation.

Making that trip, just the two of us in silence, was nothing like the way we had shopped for our tree in the past. It was so late in the season that the selection was poor. It was starting to sleet and the wind had picked up. We needed to hurry. Half-heartedly we agreed on a tree, tied it on the truck and made our way back home with it.

When we got it anchored in its stand in the den, we saw what an ugly, scrawny tree we had gotten! I quickly began hanging ornaments to cover the barest spots when I suddenly realized the lights weren't on it. Stringing the lights had always been Woody's job, and he wasn't there to do it! I sat on the floor and had a good cry. How was I to close a door when it always flew back open?

As I was struggling through that first year, there were daily first-time events which seemed insignificant but which would throw me back on a flood of memories and leave me feeling very depressed. I remember, for example, the lump in my throat and how I actually, physically, *hurt* when, for the first time, I had to say, "I'm a widow."

Even getting mail was traumatic. A letter addressed to "Mr. and Mrs." caused me to miss Woody. The first letter that came addressed just to "Mrs." made me feel alone. And when one came addressed to 'Ms.," I became angry. I just couldn't be satisfied. Everything brought memories of my loss.

Gradually I began to accept responsibilities in our Church. This was hard at first, for Woody and I had always done things together.

Church activities helped me begin living in the present. But I still felt depressed most of the time, even three years after Woody's death.

One October, Scott and Sheri, my oldest son and his wife, gave me a registration for The Beginning Experience weekend. It was there that I learned to sift out all the beautiful memories and keep them in my heart and to gently close the door on my past and to face life with new hope. By the end of that weekend, I was ready to "close the door" on my marriage.

The door that I closed has a window in it. It lets me look back on the joys, sorrows, happiness and beautiful memories. At the same time, I can look forward to my present life.

The word *mizpah* is a very special word in our

family. It is from the book of Genesis and means, "The Lord watch between me and thee while we are absent one from another." *Mizpah* is printed inside our wedding rings. It was a word we spoke to our sons, Scott and Kent, when they went to war. It was a word I used again at the end of The Beginning Experience weekend when I gently closed the door. "The Lord watch between me and thee, Woody, while we are absent one from another."

It has been five years now since Woody's death. I still miss him, but I don't live in my memories nor do I get pulled down into depression. The past is past. It is history. The present is what is here.

In the past we made a big ceremony of buying the Christmas tree. But now, in the present, we gather around the artificial tree that I bought after that first awful Christmas without Woody. Last Christmas when our family assembled, we all laughed about that scrawny tree Blake and I had picked out. I never thought I'd be able to laugh about anything connected with that first Christmas without Woody. But I can. I think Woody would be amused, too.

Reflections

"What's past is past," we say. And that's true. It's also true to say that what's past is present. It can be present in two ways: in our memories and in who we are. For, in a sense, we *are* our histories.

When the present is painful, we often like to

return to the past through our memories.

Pal did that. In that first year after Woody's death, many events drew her back into a world of memories. She seemed to think that she could keep Woody alive and keep them together in her memories. Moreover, she seemed to feel that to forget Woody would be a kind of betrayal. Therefore, to remember him constantly was a kind of loyalty.

Pal lived so vividly in the past that she sometimes "heard" Woody. Not knowing then that many widowed persons experience that type of hallucination, Pal became afraid that she was losing her sanity.

Gene, too, lives in memories of the past. He didn't "hear" Blanche, but he sometimes "spoke" to her. And he wrote to her.

Existing in the present and trying to live in the past sets up a tension that results in an almost unshakable depression. Gene tried to reason himself out of depression, and he *could* snap out of it until something reminded him again of Blanche.

Gene and Pal may have touched up their memory portraits of Blanche and Woody; but on the whole, their memories were centered on reality. The reality was that Blanche and Woody were good people and had been loving spouses.

This was not the case with Earl. He censored his memories so that only good ones were left. Even when he felt very sad, his family would be happy and smiling in the pictures he conjured up. Earl has an eye for details and natural symbols. He didn't remember just a front door; he remembered the eagle on the door and the feeling he had when he drove up to the house and saw the door.

Pal and Gene made motions of living in the present. They went to work every day and took care of their homes. But Earl did not even pretend to be interested in the present. If the ringing of his phone called him into the present, he simply put that offensive instrument into the refrigerator where the ring would be muffled. He was busy living in a different time.

Sue's attachment to the past was still different. She didn't idealize the past. She didn't select certain parts of it. Rather, she let it crowd in on her in the dark like an ancient dragon. She met this dragon of the past with two emotions: anxiety and anger.

Although Earl, Sue, Pal and Gene experienced their pasts in various ways, they shared one thing in common. They all were chained for a time in their pasts. They all lacked enthusiasm and energy for the present. Memory kept them all from moving on through their grief.

Just as they bogged down in their remembered lives in very different ways, so they also made their closures in different ways.

Pal says she finalized her closure at The Beginning Experience program. However, the very fact that she participated in the program was a sign she had *already decided* to cope with the present. An intermediate step for Pal was letting go of the guilt feelings that plagued her.

Part of the ritual in Pal's closure was the use of the word *mizpah*.

Gene ritualized his closure in the form of a letter. At the time he didn't know that letter-writing is one of the most effective and simple closure rituals. Gene had carried so many memories and so much regret inside himself that he sought a way to get it "out." He got it out on paper and then he sent the paper away.

Sue did not mention using a ritual to help her close the door on the past. She does, however, write poetry, and she has used poetry to express some of her feelings as she has tried to let go of the past. Her decision to move into the present was a decision she made gradually. The home movies were not a closure ritual but they became a sign to her that she really had let go of her anger and become detached.

It seems fitting that Earl, who lived for months so absorbed by memories of the past, should also find his symbol of closure in something he remembered. His Sheba-dog. Like Sue, Earl discovered his detachment at a simple family event. At his daughter's birthday dinner, Earl realized that he was no longer emotionally bound to Nancy. Affection didn't bind him. Neither did anger. He was free.

Closing involves opening. We don't *leave* a place without *going* to a place.

Earl and Gene, Sue and Pal left their different pasts, and they are moving into different futures. The futures they move into depend a great deal on what other closures they make, what other things they choose to leave behind.

Sue is leaving behind her tendency to let anxiety ruin her nights. She has opened doors by learning to make decisions. With surprising self-confidence, she has opened a door on a new job that offers more challenge as well as more security.

Earl has left behind his isolation and idleness. He has become more gentle in his feelings toward himself as well as toward Nancy. He has regained his sense of humor and expanded his care for people.

Gene has left behind his neat and narrow world in favor of more involvement with other hurting people. He has taken on a great deal of leadership in programs designed to help widowed and divorced people. He has chosen to exercise more compassion and to be less judgmental.

Pal has left behind her self-pity and frenzied work. She has opened the door to new hobbies and skills in sharing with others. She has learned to laugh at some of the past, like her purchase of the scrawny Christmas tree.

Laughter is perhaps one of the surest signs of new life. When we open a door and hear laughter, we know we can go in without danger.

Laughter is a sound for those appreciating the past, anticipating the future and living in the present. It is the sound of life.

5. Reaching Out to Others

Talk of reaching out to others is apt to leave an uneasy feeling that the talk is about "do-gooding." This term generally refers to those people who do good in a patronizing way. Their attitude seems to say: "We don't need any help. We have solved our problems. But, here, let us help you, you poor pitiful creature."

This chapter is not about that kind of attitude. It is about people, reaching out *from themselves* — their real selves. And these are people who have been weak and wrong, lost, selfish, hurt, hopeful.

This centering in real selves makes reaching out a human and humble experience of sharing life with others. It is hard to be patronizing with that kind of reality.

Thus when someone talks in circles, as grieving people are wont to do, people who care can listen because they, too, have thought and talked in the circle of grief. They not only *have*, but they sometimes still *do*. When someone tries to cushion their pain with drunkenness, promiscuity, bitterness or blaming, people who care can understand because they, too, have tried to blunt the sharp edge of pain. When someone seems to be making progress and then slips back into destructive behavior, people who care can be patient and encouraging because they know from their own real experience that the journey through grief is indeed a jagged journey.

There is no condescension in that kind of caring. These people do not say, "You poor thing, let me help you." They say, "Let me walk a while with you, for I know this road. I've been there. Sometimes I'm still there."

Grief is always a lonely experience. It belongs only to the one who grieves. No matter how many people have suffered losses, *this* loss is like no one else's. Others may have felt anger, but they have not felt *this* anger. In a way, then, each person can say that his or her story is different or unique.

In another way, however, there is a certain commonness to grief that brings one's life up against the lives of others who also hurt. Pain submerges people into the stream of life created by the tears of all the men and women who have ever hurt.

Once people know grief, they step into that stream of life. Those still standing on the bank cannot be present to hurting people in quite the same way grieved people can. Their own losses, then, give them both the right and the power to accompany others on their difficult roads. This is the meaning of the motto at the front of this book. Those who bear the mark of pain do indeed owe help to those who still suffer.

Being hurt is not in itself enough to qualify people to walk beside other hurting people. They must also care for themselves. They cannot understand others unless they try to understand themselves. They cannot care for others unless they care for themselves.

Caring for themselves means that they claim their need for understanding and affection and that they give themselves permission to ask for those things. It means that they unburden themselves from guilt by forgiving themselves and accepting God's forgiveness. It means that they give themselves time, that they are hopeful in the expectations they set for themselves and patient in their failures to meet those expectations. Above all, it means that they are gentle.

Closure on the past means openness to the present. People who are ready to make a new beginning need to see and hear and feel and interpret events and people in the here-and-now. Their own experience of loss can serve as a kind of spiritual radar which detects pain in others.

To respond to the needs of themselves and of others is perhaps the surest way to close the door on the past and to begin anew. Their reaching out to others is life-giving because both caring and being cared for helps them feel more alive.

Earl's Story

In order for me to care for others, I first had to start

caring for myself. And to do that, I had to become more understanding.

Before my own divorce, I didn't understand the divorce situation. I had never let myself get close enough. The one or two times that people I knew got a divorce, I was quick to turn my back on them. I felt it was their fault and that if they had used a little sense, it would not have happened. Now I think I really didn't want to think about divorced people because down deep I knew it could happen to me; and just the possibility of it was enough to make me turn my back on these people and their situations.

Several divorced men worked for me when I was married. In looking back, I realize that these men were among the best help I had. I didn't understand why they were so quick to suggest working on holidays and weekends when it wasn't necessary. One of these men begged me to let him work on Christmas day because he had no other place to go or anything else to do. I didn't understand that these men needed to be told that they were needed.

Being married and having a business of my own made me eligible to give these men advice! I can remember how mad I would get when they would get drunk and come to work hung over. I would tell them it was my business because it affected the way they worked.

One man had a little boy the same age as my youngest son, Jay. At times, this man would mope around and tell me how good his boy was and how much he missed him. I finally told him that he might just as well forget his son because his ex-wife would soon marry and his son would have a new daddy. Those words of mine still ring in my ears, and I am really ashamed for not being more understanding.

If I ever see these men again—especially the man who felt so bad about his son—I will tell them I'm sorry. I wasn't caring because I wasn't understanding.

My divorce has helped me to find out a lot about myself that I didn't know before. I never realized what a sensitive person I am. I always hid my feelings, even from myself. I can't hide them anymore, and I don't even want to.

I can see some of the change in myself by the way I am more understanding of the men who now work for me.

Last Fourth of July weekend, I decided to work. The divorced man and the two married men working for me agreed to come to work. But come Saturday morning, only the divorced man showed up. We couldn't do the job without more help. So when a Mexican boy stopped and asked if I could hire two friends of his, I told him to have them there by 9 o'clock. At exactly nine, they showed up.

I almost sent them home! The Mexican boy who had brought them introduced them as Marcos and Ciro. I later learned that Ciro, who was 18 and had two kids, and Marcos, who was 31 and had five kids, were cousins. They had left Mexico and swum the Rio Bravos to come to America to make money to send back to their families.

I looked at Marcos and decided he was small but

could maybe do some light work. Then I looked down at Ciro who is 5'1" and weighs 123 pounds. He looked to be around 14. He just stared at the ground. I decided I'd go ahead and try to use them for the four-day holiday. I asked if either one spoke English. When I said "English," Marcos said, "No."

I then had to laugh. Here I was trying to go back to work after not working for so long and I end up with a crew like this!

I thought for a minute and then went to the pickup and got two shovels. I handed one to Marcos and one to Ciro. I pointed and said, "Shovel." Marcos quickly told me the word back in Spanish. There we were having a language lesson! I repeated the word in Spanish and gently pushed them toward the work area. I told myself I was going to pay dearly for working on this Fourth of July.

I was soon amazed, however, at the amount of work that those two men could do! I was almost sorry I'd have to let them go at the end of the holiday weekend.

That afternoon I was working under a pipe with a large wrench and I tried to get Ciro to help me hold it up. He couldn't understand what I was saying and I got a little impatient. He turned around and went to the back of the bore pit and stood there with his head hung down. He wouldn't look up.

As I looked at him, I felt ashamed of myself and sorry for him. He was out of place in a world that was new and strange to him. I suddenly realized how he must feel, because I too, had had the feeling I was in a new and strange world. I, too, had heard things I just couldn't comprehend, even though the words had been in English! I had stood in the pit of life not wanting to look up.

I went to Ciro, took him by the arm with as much kindness as I could, and then I pointed, grunted and grinned him into helping me. That was the last time I lost patience with either one of them.

Needless to say, when Wednesday came, I didn't let them go. I kept them on the job, and gave them a raise!

The third day Marcos and Ciro worked for me, their ride failed to pick them up. When I came to work the next morning, I saw that they had spent the night in the pit without food or water. The way they scampered out of the pit like two small rats almost made me cry! And I had thought life was so hard on me. From that moment, I was determined to help them all I could. I started picking them up and taking them home, even though it took an extra hour and a half every day. They would never have to sleep on the job again.

With what little Spanish I learned while growing up in New Mexico, and with their being such good teachers and quick learners, we have learned to communicate with a little Spanish, a little English, and a whole lot of hand talk. Marcos wants to be called Mark. We didn't know an English version of Ciro, so he decided to be called Jimmy.

My Mom and Dad have a little garage apartment at their house and, with me telling them what a fine pair of people Jimmy and Mark were, they agreed to rent to them. Jimmy and Mark were tickled to death. When we don't work on weekends, I sometimes drop over to see if they need anything.

I do more for Jimmy and Mark than I do for myself. I buy their clothes and take them to the store and I even take them to the laundromat! Now that's something I don't do for myself.

I can't help comparing my feelings for Jimmy and Mark with the way I felt toward the men who worked for me before my divorce. I understand a lot more now.

Jimmy and Mark have done a lot to help me rebuild meaning in my life and care for people. But the person who has helped me most is my youngest son, Jay. He is now seven. My other two children are older and too busy to stay with me. Not Jay.

Now when I feel myself getting down, I call and go get Jay. Between the two of us, we discuss a lot of problems. We go to bed early and talk. He tells me about the disadvantages of being a little person and I tell him of all the advantages. They may not be able to drive cars, but when they trip, they don't have far to fall. We snuggle till he has trouble breathing.

In the mornings, while he is still in a dead sleep, I look at him. He sleeps with his mouth open and with a look of pure innocence. One front tooth has outgrown the other. His little corncob feet with broken toenails have seen a lot of summer. He claims the fresh cut on his knee took 11 stitches, but I know it took only seven. My other two call me Daddy; he calls me Dad.

When I get to feeling down and wonder why I even try to work and straighten out my life, I think of my kids.

As I have learned to be more understanding of myself and others, I have been able to let go of some of my anger.

I am now not so angry with women because I've met so many good women. I've become real friends with some of these women and we talk and share a lot. I can understand their pain.

I'm not as angry with preachers and priests as I was for so many years. When I was young, the old parish priest used to humiliate me till I would almost be in tears. In front of our whole class, he would call me stupid when I couldn't tell him what the Sunday sermon had been about. I can remember sitting there smiling hard just to keep from crying.

As I grew older, my fear turned to anger and dislike. I went for years with this feeling until I had the chance to meet some preachers and priests as men. They didn't come on with *"Mea culpas"* and "I'm a-tellin' you, brothers." They were people like me whose job was different. With openness on both sides, I have managed to let go of the hard feelings I had for so long. Coy is one of the finest men I know. It just so happens that his business is preaching!

I could never say I'm glad my divorce happened. It hurt my kids too much. And it hurt me. But I can say that since my divorce, I have discovered some good things in myself that I didn't realize before. I understand a whole lot more, so I care a whole lot more. Life is too short to spend it being angry. I don't think I could ever see someone hurt again and not care.

Pal's Story

In the Hindu language, the word *widow* means empty. For so long, that's the way I felt: *empty.* Everything I did was done from habit or routine. Life was mechanical. People talked; I heard their voices, but I didn't listen. As long as I was empty myself, I couldn't reach out to others.

The office where I worked was a 30-minute drive from home. Very early each morning, I'd put my lunch on the car seat beside me and begin my drive. I took the same route every day—out MacArthur Boulevard and then east to Edmond. MacArthur was badly in need of repairs and, after many trips, my car was badly in need of repairs, too.

One day, a friend asked me why I took that route. It was longer and rougher than going down Meridian. When I thought of her question, I realized that for months I drove down MacArthur to avoid driving by the cemetery where Woody was buried. My action was mechanical. In a way, it seems like I was guarding my emptiness.

I think it was during those early morning drives that I began to care for myself. As I drove, the sun would peek over the horizon and paint the sky with splashes of pinks, purples and yellows. I'd wish for my palette and brush. The whole sky seemed full of peace. It was a perfect time for reflection on my life and on my relationship with God. I prayed a lot as I bounced over MacArthur's chuckholes.

As I prayed I thought of how Jesus had cried out in anguish on the cross. I remembered that he had cried when his friend Lazarus died. It was as if God was saying to me, "It's okay to cry and to ask for help." Up until then I was trying to work everything out by myself, trying to appear strong for the sake of the children. I still had felt that there was something incompatible between faith and grief.

In time, I began talking more freely about my feelings to the children. When I talked to Blake, he seemed embarrassed, but he also seemed to understand. I tried not to cry in front of him. Maybe that was wrong; I don't know.

Kathy and Craig would often stop by after work, and we'd sit around the kitchen table drinking coffee or Cokes. Craig frequently rubbed my neck and shoulders as I talked, and I could feel the tension slipping away. Many times I shed tears. By reaching out to them, I was caring for myself, and this helped ease my emptiness and loneliness.

One Saturday afternoon, Irene stopped by. Irene is a friend of mine who is also widowed. She listened that afternoon while I poured out my frustrations, my doubts and fears. She assured me that I wasn't losing my sanity, and she told me there would come a time when thoughts of Woody would not occupy almost all my waking hours. She held my hand and that touch told me she understood. I needed her understanding. I had to care enough for myself to let her care for me. This was a humbling experience for me.

When I attended The Beginning Experience weekend, I met other widowed and divorced people. They were so willing to listen when I talked. I was even able to talk about my sexual frustrations. The look in their eyes told me they understood and their hands on my arm said they wanted to walk with me on my journey back to peace.

Going through the pain of grief has given me insight into the suffering of divorced people as well as of widowed people. It has also helped me realize that I can help others because I understand and I can *listen*. Listening was a gift to me. It's also a gift I can give to others.

One evening a few months ago, I picked up the phone to make a business call. I didn't sit down because this was to be a quick call. But very soon, I knew this call was different. The person on the other end of the line was desperately in need of someone to talk to. His wife was divorcing him.

Because of my own loss, I was able to understand his pain. I was able to share some of my own feelings, but I mostly listened. As the minutes ticked by and the conversation went from business to his personal grief, I pulled up a chair. The clock ticked on. Twenty minutes. Thirty minutes. By now my hand and ear were numb and I moved the receiver to the other hand and other ear. There were to be more exchanges of the receiver as I continued to listen. He shed many tears and after more than an hour, he said he felt a weight lifted from his shoulders. He thanked me. All I had done was listen.

Recently my daughter-in-law, Sheri, had major surgery. When she returned home, she wasn't able to lift her baby or do any housework. She felt helpless and stranded. I went over often and took care of the baby and the house. But I know that my major help was understanding. When I saw the look of frustration in Sheri's eyes when she saw all there was to do and couldn't do it, I knew the feeling. It was something like the way I had felt when I saw life going on but I couldn't seem to live it!

My life has changed a lot since Woody's death. Some of the things that were of primary importance when I was married have lost a lot of their appeal. My needs and interests are different. I wonder what Woody would say if he saw the change in me. I think he would like it.

I'm sharing more of my life with others who need a smile, a handshake, or a visit. I am not relying so much on my children for companionship. I cherish my old friendships. I have also made a broad circle of new friends who include people of all faiths and all walks of life. I'm sure that our Creator has plans for me to carry on with life and to reach out to others. Otherwise, why would he have left me here when at one time I would rather have died?

I'm not empty any more. I'm Pal and I happen to be a widow.

Sue's Story

Spring had finally come to Minnesota. The blossoming of the trees and flowers added just the right touch to the style show we had planned. Crepe paper decorations inside the cafeteria at Rochester's state mental hospital brightened the sterile atmosphere. The clothes modeled by the patients accented the theme of spring with bright and airy colors and fabrics. The most beautiful of all the sights that day were the smiles on the faces of women who, a few short months before, seemed to have forgotten how to smile.

I was proud to be one of the volunteers who had helped with the sewing class for these women. They knew me as one of the "Mrs. Jaycees" who had come to the hospital for several months and helped them cut, sew and plan for this event. I felt good about the work we had done together, but I never revealed anything about myself while working with the group.

It was different with Alice. When I began working with her on a one-to-one basis, our relationship was a personal one. Alice was a thin woman in her late 50's. She had sad, deep-set eyes and her dark hair hung down loosely about her shoulders. She had been a patient at the hospital for 30 years with no family to visit her or to take her for short excursions into the world outside the hospital grounds.

Although Alice was unable to communicate her feelings to me verbally, I knew something of the loneliness she must have felt. We had recently moved far away from family and friends and I, too, was lonely. When we went out to go shopping, Alice would become confused by the people and the noise. I related to that feeling because I, too, had experienced some confusion and uneasiness when thrust into unfamiliar surroundings. And I understood her excitement as she waited impatiently for my visits, pestering the nurses persistently until she saw me coming down the corridor.

With Alice I was not just playing the role of helper. I was her friend.

As a "helper" in the sewing class, I was acting out a familiar pattern — playing roles. When I was a child I filled the role of good student and near-perfect daughter, hoping to win approval and diminish the possibility of rejection. In marriage, I tried to fill the role of good wife. In later years, I automatically assumed roles such as mother, Sunday school teacher and volunteer. Not that I wasn't being honest. I *wanted* to be a good mother and teacher and wife. But I always looked for "models" to see how to do these things. I hid the real Sue behind the roles. I knew of no role that fit me as a divorced person. There was no mask I could put on to hide my fear and depression from those around me.

Looking back over those times, I now see that God was working in my life even though I felt totally alone. He knew that I would need the love and support of others to begin the long climb out of those depths of depression. It was at the time of my greatest need that Joan, Judith, Tom and other friends extended their hands to me. With their encouragement, I began to learn to live again.

For a long time my idea of helping others had been that of being a giver — giving my time, energy and love. Taking from others made me uncomfortable. When I was in the position of having to accept help I felt unable to give anything in return. But now I see helping and caring as a two-way street. Others helped me. And now I can help others in a way that is much more satisfying than the way I used to help. Now it's Sue, not a role. Helping is a two-way sharing.

Because I was able to *take* the love and care of others, I've learned to accept the fact that I am lovable. This is still the most difficult thing for me to believe. It's even hard for me to write this because, for so many years the one thing of which I was totally sure was my worthlessness.

When I realized that people love me as I truly am and not for what they expect me to be, I decided to start searching for the goodness they saw in me. I have discovered some good things about Sue in my search. God has given me a good mind and a tender heart. Sometimes almost too tender — as the number of stray animals around our house will bear out! I am dependable, except when it comes to writing letters. I have a good sense of humor and I love to laugh. I haven't entirely overcome my negative self-image, but I have come a long way towards accepting myself as someone who can be loved.

I find I can help my friends because I have personal knowledge of the pain and frustration they are feeling. I know the loneliness and confusion that comes with being single again. When I need someone to share my feelings with, they are the people to whom I turn for help because they understand. They have been there.

Teresa is one such friend. She is divorced and has four children at home. She can relate to the problems of being a single parent, working full time

166

and trying to provide the love and care children need.

Last weekend Teresa and I went to see "The Goodbye Girl." The show was thoroughly enjoyable and we were both reluctant to end our night on the town. I invited her over for a while so we could talk. My children were asleep, so Teresa and I stumbled through the living room in the dark and I turned on the light in the kitchen. We sat together at the table, talking and laughing until midnight.

Our conversation turned to our children and we shared some of the anxieties and hopes we had in dealing with the responsibilities of being single parents. I was encouraged to hear her voice doubts about how to discipline her children and how to provide them with a good example consistently, even when she had had a bad day at work and was tired and discouraged. I related to her anxieties and told her I have similar doubts.

This kind of sharing is what I mean by a two-way street. Teresa and I trust each other to understand the feelings we each express without fearing we'll be excused with a word of sage advice or judged as an unwise parent. My heart was lighter when Teresa left that night and I'm sure hers was too.

The past three years have not been easy for me and I would never want to relive them, but I have gained much from them. Now, when I reach out to another person who is hurting, I do so as I did with Alice. I reach out as a friend, as someone who has a personal knowledge of pain and of the joy that can come when life is reborn because of that pain.

Gene's Story

I often say that I have led a charmed life. Without my putting a lot into it, the good things just happened. I had nothing to do with where or to whom I was born, how I was raised, or how I inherited Christian faith. I had very little to do with the timing of my military service or the government grant that paid for my college education. The ultimate in my good fortune, though, was falling in love with Blanche and sharing 25 years of my life with her.

I needed help many years ago when I was in the service. I was careless one time, and I got drunk. Good and proper. That has been the only experience of drunkenness in my life, and it was sufficient. I pulled that stunt off so splendidly that I made up for all the opportunities I had missed up to that point, and it was more than enough to carry me right on through the rest of my life, no matter how long I might live. It was brutal.

In the drinking process on that memorable occasion, I reached a point where I knew I had consumed too much; but I tried to force myself to act as if I still had everything in control. I failed miserably. I lost control of myself and eventually passed out. Although I didn't know it at the time because of my condition, I was in great need of help.

Luckily help was there. Two of my buddies managed to get me back to the barracks, put me in my bunk and care for me until the fog in my brain cleared. For sure, my composure "act" was over. I had to admit that I was hurting and needed the help of my buddies.

In kind of the same way, I was knocked from my senses by the tragedy that came to our family in Blanche's death. It, too, was brutal! I had never before had to cope with a loss of such magnitude. I tried to lead others to believe that I was holding up very well. Really, though, I could feel my emotional equilibrium breaking down. My concentrated efforts to stabilize myself only left me dizzier and more confused. I needed help, but I didn't want it to show.

Once again, however, help was there when I needed it.

This time, the help came from total strangers. They accepted me and showed they cared simply because they understood my kind of hurt. I had to admit that I had failed at trying to get through my grief by myself and that I needed help. Help came from caring people in a support group called The Beginning Experience.

Just who were these people who ministered to me for no other reason than because they cared? They weren't counselors or psychiatrists. They weren't doctors, hypnotists or specialists trained to lead people out of depression. They were people involved in The Beginning Experience. Like me, they knew the experience of hurt, frustration and confusion that comes from a deep loss. Some of them were widowed and could identify with me so closely. Some were married or single people who cared and who knew loss, even though it wasn't loss of a spouse. Most of them were divorced. I was most surprised to find that it was the divorced people who were so quick to respond to my silent cry for help, to detect the pain I felt behind my composure act.

I had never been close to a divorce situation before, and I had never really stopped to think about what it would be like to be divorced from a once-loved person. Before this, when I would hear about someone getting a divorce, I would usually say something trite like, "Oh, they could have made it work if they had tried," or, "It's their own damned fault; they're probably getting what they deserve." And that would end it for me. No thought or concern for the pain that I have now come to realize is present in the majority of cases.

It seemed strange to me that, in my own grief, these were some of the people who were so caring for me. Despite their own pain, they could reach out and care for others. I discovered that I could also reach out, and I was amazed to discover that I, too, possessed some magic in my touch.

I came to realize that I have always had my share of human feelings, but for so much of my life, I had let only a few know or see them. I began to want to take a closer look at my feelings and to see them for what they really are and not for what someone else expects them to be. I want to be honest with myself and rip off the old masks that cover up the real me.

Once I began to face myself and to risk reaching out to others, I found my life becoming more life-giving. I had greatly missed being able to care for Blanche, and now I found that there were so many people I could care for. I had missed telling Blanche my innermost thoughts and feelings, and now there were so many people willing to absorb as much as I cared to express. I had missed Blanche's closeness, her touches, her physical being, and here were so many longing for those very same things.

I couldn't hold it in; I found that I really cared that others were hurting as I was, or much more. I saw and heard their expressions, their struggles to get their feelings out, their sobs — and I understood.

Besides not sharing my general feelings in the past, I had not been able to express appreciation about the good things I noticed in others. I began risking in this area, too. I wonder now why I was so afraid to do this all those years.

It seems to me that most of the human race is the same — afraid, ashamed and embarrassed about having feelings. So often, it seems to me, feelings make only a brief appearance at highly emotional times such as weddings and funerals. And then, once those events are over, back the feelings go into the deep recesses of the mind. I don't want to let that happen to me. Now that I have let my feelings out into the sunlight, I never want them to slip back into the shadows again.

Putting my feelings down in writing has been quite a revelation to me. I have written some notes and letters that have been so well received that I am astounded. I don't know why I am surprised, though, for I know that some of the written messages I've received have been very special and encouraging to me.

A written message can be kept alive and real as if

the person who wrote it is uniquely present, saying those things over and over. My greatest treasure is the last written message I received from Blanche. The occasion was a milestone birthday that I reached just a few months before she died — a birthday I wasn't too happy to see come! In her pretty script, Blanche wrote just two brief sentences: "To me you will always be young. I love you. Blanche." God, I am thankful she *wrote* those words instead of just thinking them or saying them.

When I think of the importance of sharing feelings, I can't help thinking of how I have so thoroughly failed to do this during so many years of my life. Because of my narrowed outlook, I have failed to see, hear and understand other people. It has taken the experience of my own deep loss to open my eyes.

Some years ago my sister Louise was divorced. It's only now that I can begin to comprehend the bitter struggles and frustrations that she went through — all alone. Without even me. To her, I say: "I am sorry; I just didn't understand then."

To my friends Sue and Earl who have bared their souls in these pages and who just happen to be divorced, I say, "Thank you for caring. You and so many like you are truly 'wounded healers.' Just by being yourselves, by acknowledging your grief and by your determination to make it just one more day, I have seen what that familiar pain is like from a different viewpoint. Because of you, I have been encouraged and guided in my own grief."

Now I want to learn to be more caring for others and to show my care. I want to establish friendships that are on a feeling level. I want to share in my friends' happiness as well as in their sorrows. I want to trust and be trusted. I want no more loneliness. A little solitude and silence is fine, but no loneliness.

I once received a little scroll that had a most meaningful message written on it: "Those of us who bear the mark of pain are never really free, for we owe a debt to those who are still hurting." I believe in those words. I have been marked with pain and I know now that I can make that pain a life-giving gift for others. I want to do that.

A charmed life once again is mine.

Reflections

At the beginning of this book, four people stood at the far edge of grief. Grief yawned before them like a dark cave. They hung back at the entrance of that cave because they were not sure they would make it through all the night-like twists and turns and finally find their way to light on the other side. Entering the cave seemed too much like dying; the cave seemed too much like a tomb. And so they balked. That is where we met them—Sue, Earl, Pal and Gene—stunned and denying at the beginning of their passage through grief.

Now at the end of the book, we see the same four people emerging into light and new life. With rare candor they have told us about their difficult passages through grief. In the telling, they have also unconsciously told us about another journey: one that led to the deepest places inside themselves. Profound sorrow sent them on these winding interior journeys where they discovered *more* of the persons they had always potentially been.

Thus the Sue, Gene, Pal and Earl we see at the end of the book seem changed. Grief did not change them; they changed themselves by discovering and using new goodnesses and strengths.

Not only did they find unexpected qualities, but also—and this was the frightening thing!—they failed to find some of the old stand-by strengths they thought would help them make their twisting journeys through grief.

All four of them went through the typical stages of grief—denial, anger, loneliness and depression. The differences in their lives—as in the lives of all who pass through grief—were made in their discoveries and use of new-life qualities.

When Pal stood at the brink of the dark cave, she looked into herself to find the old faith that enabled her to deny grief. She did not find it. She looked to find peace in being single as she had found peace in being married. Peace wasn't there. She looked for busyness to quiet her body and dull her frustrations, but it simply exhausted her and brought her loneliness to a higher pitch. Pal could not make the trip through pain with her old strengths because they seemed to have abandoned her at the entrance. She had to go deeper inside herself to find other strengths.

She discovered independence, enriched faith and a stronger outreach.

All her life up to that point, Pal had been "the

daughter of," "the wife of," or "the mother of." She did not know that she could simply be Pal. With Woody gone and her children mostly grown, she was alone for the first time. Life called her to use a quality of independence that she had left more or less unused.

She accepted the challenge. Pal now manages the house, takes cares of repairs, makes new friends, goes places and does things without depending on someone else to help her decide. She does things as Pal, not just as wife or mother. Her independence also enabled her to step beyond the somewhat restricted world of relatives and fellow parishioners and to form new friendships with people who are different from her in background and in outlook.

Pal also found a richer faith inside herself. It was not the kind of faith that took away her grief, but it was the more mature kind which enabled her to claim her pain and to cope with it.

Pal also found a concern for others that led her to reach out to more people. Pal had cared, of course, for her children and for Woody. She had cared for other people, too; but she had not shared herself with them. Her habit of demure reticence had kept her at a distance.

Life now called her to new levels of trust and compassion. Now when Pal listens to a business acquaintance on the phone talk about the pain of going through a divorce, she can both empathize with him and share her own experience.

Of the four persons who have told their stories here, Sue was probably most surprised at the new-life qualities which she found within herself.

Her main expectation was that her almost scrupulous attendance to certain moral values would keep some semblance of order in her life. That expectation failed her. And Sue thought she had nothing left but her old weaknesses of dependency, insecurity and indecisiveness. So when pain pushed her not only into grief but also into her inward journey, she balked. She could not go because she had no strength! She considered suicide. She resisted the help of a psychiatrist and tried, literally, to block his words out of her consciousness.

When Sue finally looked within herself, she found a steely strength that surprised her. She was able to let go of destructive behavior. Today Sue confidently takes care of a challenging job. She creates a stable home. She sleeps at nights without being overtaken by regrets and anxieties.

Probably the most important discovery that Sue made—and the most difficult one for her to claim—was her own unique goodness. She had always felt worthless. Today, however, Sue can look in the mirror and say, "You, Sue Carpenter, are a good woman."

This new self-esteem is one of the qualities which enables Sue to reach out to others with quiet compassion and with frank sharing of her own feelings. When Sue sat in the kitchen talking with her friend Teresa at midnight about the anxieties of being a single parent, Sue was not just "helping" or "feeling sorry"; she was sharing.

Despite her busy schedule, Sue finds time to reach out to others by helping to direct a diocesan parenting program. She also helped to create a special weekend program for children who have lost a parent through death or divorce.

Sue can do these things and find joy in life because deep inside herself she found strength, self-esteem and a special compassion for hurting children.

When Earl stood at the beginning of grief, he thought he could be stoic. He had always handled difficult feelings by being tough or by stifling them. If all else failed, surely work would see him through. But Earl found neither stoicism nor the old drive to work. Those qualities he had always counted on seemed to vanish.

So Earl hung back. He tried to avoid both the journey through grief and the journey into himself. If he couldn't call on his natural toughness with which to face life, he would simply avoid facing it. He tried to blot it out by drinking and sleeping. Perhaps he could make his way through grief in a kind of stupor.

But Earl's finer qualities kept knocking at his consciousness. He finally began his inward trek. He found inside himself a world of rich feelings. He claimed them all—those that hurt him as well as those that gladdened him. Among those feelings, he discovered an unusually sensitive compassion for people—particularly for people most likely to be overlooked. His compassion, combined with a Mark Twain wit, enables Earl to touch others in a way that invites honesty and growth.

Earl discovered a moral toughness that enables him to be honest and to begin changing his destructive behavior. At first Earl tried not to face reality, but now he faces it with honesty. He has stopped using alcohol as a crutch. His moral toughness has enabled him to begin working again and to begin the long process of paying off his debts. Once in a while Earl becomes discouraged. The journey still seems so long, the debts so unending. But his new kind of toughness helps him to straighten his back and keep at his job.

Earl discovered a faith in God that he thought he had abandoned. He has a natural religious inclination. He is still suspicious of too much ceremony and too many legalities, but he now claims God simply as his friend.

Earl's recently tapped compassion and honest faith have led him to become involved in helping others who are going through grief. Until recently, Earl would not write a letter or fill out a questionnaire. In the past year, he has written numerous talks which he has presented for both local and national groups. He has been very involved with The Beginning Experience in Oklahoma City.

Gene, too, experienced the temporary loss of old strengths and the discovery of new ones. He expected his even-tempered patience to keep some smoothness in his life. He both surprised and disappointed himself by becoming impatient and short-tempered over insignificant things. He thought the regularity of his life would carry him back into his habitual contentment. He thought his faith would bring him swiftly to peace. But Gene found neither contentment nor peace. Routine was empty and faith seemed uncomforting.

What Gene did find was an unexpected quality of flexibility. When life had been marked by stability and routine, Gene had not needed flexibility. Now he did. Gene has changed because he has *stretched* his faith, his life-style, his circle of friends, his involvements, his values.

Gene has become a real friend—not just a friendly acquaintance—with people he would not have even had occasion to meet in his old pattern of life. In the past, Gene was inclined to be unsympathetic and judgmental toward people who were divorced or who lived according to values different from his own. Now Gene is understanding, empathetic, genuinely interested and caring. Gene has taken on leadership responsibilities in The Beginning Experience on both local and national levels.

It seems as if Gene has even stretched his sense of humor. It is still gentle, but it is quicker and keener.

Life, or pain in life, has called Earl, Sue, Pal and Gene to use new-life powers within themselves. Loss came to them. They had to make a choice at that point either to withdraw from the pain or to enter into it. In a way, it was a choice between death or life.

To withdraw from the journey of grief and the journey inside themselves would be to die spiritually and emotionally. To make the journeys would be to find life. New life. They chose life.

This choice is what we mean by the abstract-sounding term "the power of the resurrection." The historical experience of Jesus contains a promise that each of us *can* pass through pain and find our own resurrection, our own new life. Over and over again. With each loss (which is a kind of death) we can find new life.

That power is within us because God is within us.

Different people find different new-life qualities. Pal found independence. Sue discovered self-esteem. Earl found talent and moral toughness. Gene found flexibility. *All* of them found compassion. That is one new-life quality that seems common to all who pass through grief. Perhaps that is why these widowed and divorced persons seem so amazingly sensitive in their reaching out to others.

We saw only glimpses of their reaching out: Pal helping her daughter-in-law or listening to a friend on the phone; Sue in her kitchen at midnight talking with a friend; Gene at his desk writing his sister Louise to tell her that he finally understood her pain; Earl in his pickup truck taking Mark and Jimmy to the laundromat. In all these glimpses there is the mark of new life. For—and this is the important point—the power of the resurrection takes place where we live. We may *reflect* on it in churches, but we *live* it in kitchens and offices and bore pits.

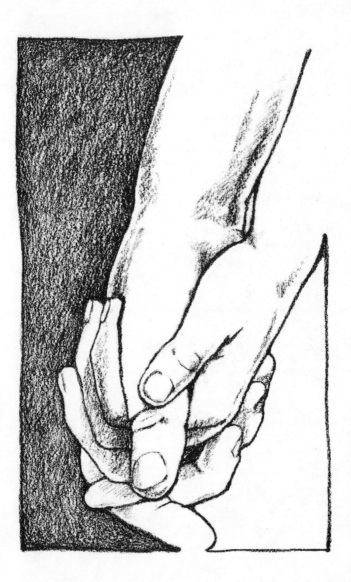

Postscript

The Beginning Experience began to evolve at—of all things—a Marriage Encounter. Sister Josephine Stewart and a good friend of hers, Jo Lamia, who was divorced, attended a Marriage Encounter in October of 1973. Both Josephine and Jo were involved with various retreat and personal-growth programs in the diocese of Fort Worth, Texas, and Marriage Encounter was one of the diocesan programs. During the weekend, Jo was moved to write her former husband a gentle letter of closure. That letter was the seed which grew into The Beginning Experience.

The impact of the letter and the dialogue which followed helped Josephine, a marriage and family counselor, see the importance of making a firm and gentle closure on the past in order to move more fully into the present.

Josephine and Gail Smith, director of the Catholic Renewal Center of North Texas, wrote the original outline for The Beginning Experience during the summer of 1974. The pilot weekend was held in October, 1974. The response to that weekend quickly indicated that The Beginning Experience was destined to be more than a local program.

Twenty states now offer The Beginning Experience program. The national office is at 4503 Bridge Street, Fort Worth, Texas 76103.